THE SMALLEST ONES

THE SMALLEST ONES

Two sisters' escape from
DRC rebels and their pursuit
of freedom

POPINA KHUMANDA

PENGUIN BOOKS

The Smallest Ones

Published by Penguin Books
an imprint of Penguin Random House South Africa (Pty) Ltd
Reg. No. 1953/000441/07
The Estuaries No. 4, Oxbow Crescent, Century Avenue, Century City, 7441
PO Box 1144, Cape Town, 8000, South Africa
www.penguinrandomhouse.co.za

Penguin
Random House
South Africa

First published 2025

1 3 5 7 9 10 8 6 4 2

PUBLISHER: Marlene Fryer
MANAGING EDITOR: Robert Plummer
EDITOR: Nicola Rijsdijk
COVER DESIGNER: Ryan Africa
TYPESETTER: Monique van den Berg

Set in 11.5 pt on 16.5 pt Adobe Garamond Pro

Printed by **novus print**, a division of Novus Holdings

MIX
Paper | Supporting
responsible forestry
FSC
www.fsc.org   FSC® C022948

ISBN 978 1 77639 220 9 (print)
ISBN 978 1 77639 221 6 (ePub)

Some names have been changed to protect the identity of those involved.

To Lola: Not even our gods can separate us.

And to YaZiana: Together, we are not just chasing freedom — we are building it, brick by brick, with every step we take.

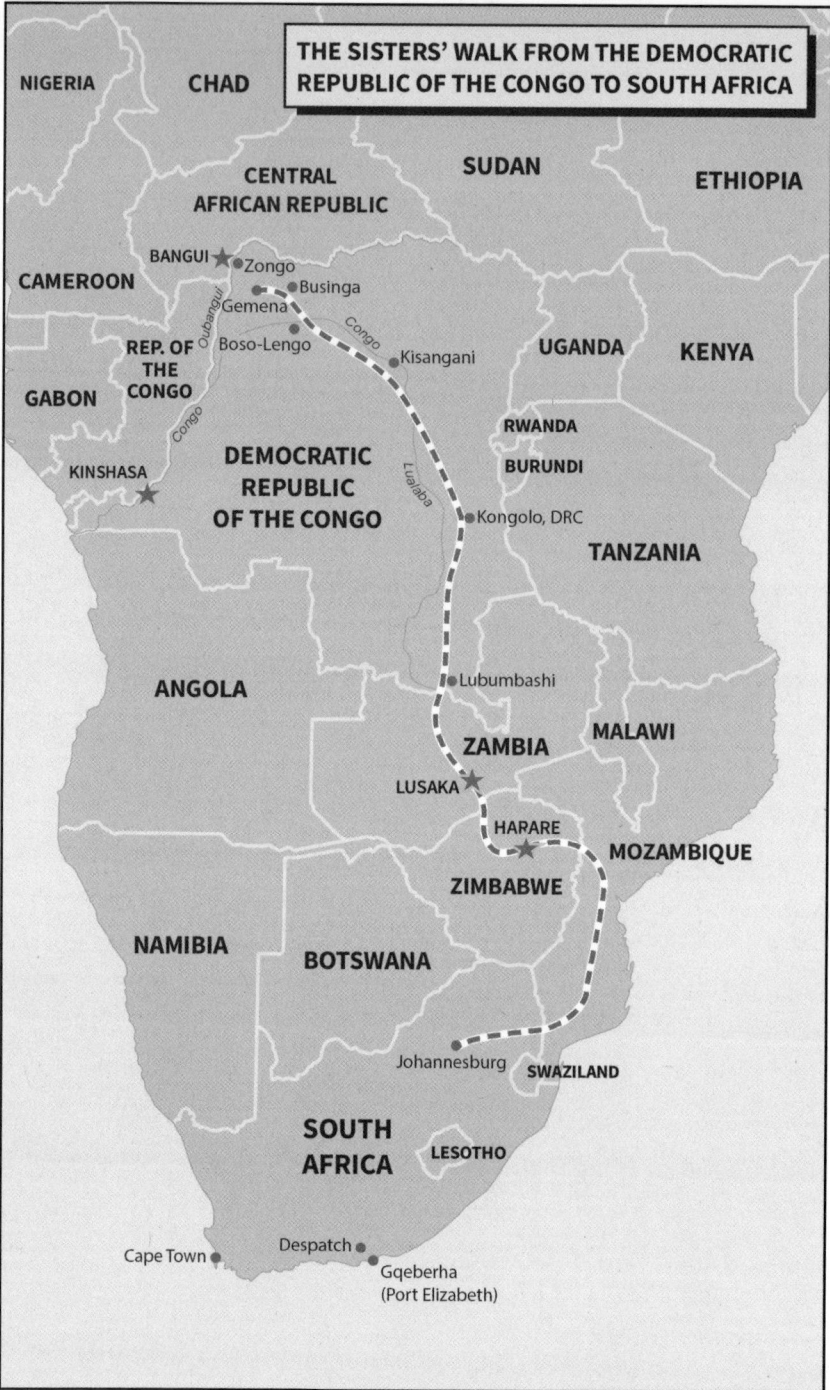

THE SISTERS' WALK FROM THE DEMOCRATIC
REPUBLIC OF THE CONGO TO SOUTH AFRICA

Preface

Freedom, I have come to understand, isn't just the absence of chains or oppression. It's about being able to make choices, to find opportunities and be empowered to act on them. To grow as a person. As a child in my four-month walk across the DRC to South Africa and during the many struggles that followed, I learnt that true freedom doesn't come from comfort or privilege – it's crafted from the struggle for a better life. That's why I originally called this book "Building Freedom" – because freedom is built by active choices, every day, step by step.

Building freedom is not for the faint-hearted. It requires vision to look beyond your circumstances, no matter how dire. The path to true independence isn't just about escaping trauma – it's about creating a future where I can choose who it is I become. In this way, I've come to see that the many struggles I faced aren't meaningless – they have shaped me and pushed me to dream, even when things seemed impossible. The nightmares about my past may have ended, but my dreams remain. And while yesterday's pain still lingers, so does the hope of tomorrow.

I hope my story inspires you to find your own path to freedom, to build it even when the odds seem stacked against you. May my story give hope to every voiceless girl who hasn't been allowed to dream, to every woman who has endured abuse and forgotten who she is and what she is capable of, to every soul yearning for a better life but not knowing where to start.

As humans, we were made to be free. And freedom starts with the simple decision to believe.

*

I first stepped into a school when I was twelve years old, and it has been a dream come true to be able to write this book.

The moment I first held my schoolbooks and stationery, I fell in love with reading and writing. It became my way of connecting with the world. *The Smallest Ones* is more than just a book for me – it represents a journey of healing, acceptance, a rediscovery of who I am and where I come from.

Writing this book has not only allowed me to confront my own experiences but has also given me the courage to speak out for countless women and children in the DRC who face unimaginable hardships every day. Their stories, like mine, are often filled with pain, but also with resilience, hope and a deep yearning for freedom.

While I was writing, I was studying and battling the depths of depression. There were days when I wanted to hide from the world, feeling utterly vulnerable and broken. Yet life kept pushing me forward. I had to put on a brave face, get up every morning and go to work as if everything was fine, as if the weight of my story wasn't slowly consuming me.

There were nights when I cried until dawn, reliving memories that I had tried so hard to bury. The act of writing, though cathartic, often felt like it was taking every bit of life out of me. But even in those moments, I realised the importance of telling my truth.

This book is not just a reflection of my journey but is also a testament to the strength it takes to rebuild yourself, bit by bit, after everything falls apart. It's for the women and children of the DRC, and for anyone who has ever felt silenced or lost.

This is my offering – a story of survival, resilience and the unwavering pursuit of freedom.

Historical context

The Democratic Republic of the Congo (DRC) has a long and complex history of rebellion. Since the country's independence from Belgium in 1960, numerous groups have sought to challenge the government and gain autonomy.

The first major uprising was the Simba rebellion, which was active between 1963 and 1965, led by the Congolese National Liberation Front (FLNC). Although it was initially successful in taking control of large parts of the country, the rebellion was eventually defeated by government forces and the FLNC disbanded. The next major events were the Shaba I and Shaba II rebellions in 1977 and 1978, led by the Front for the National Liberation of the Congo (FNLC). These were aimed at overthrowing the government of Mobutu Sese Seko, who had taken power in 1965 and renamed the country the Republic of Zaire in 1971. The FNLC took control of parts of the territory but eventually disbanded after its defeat by government forces.

Violence in the country continued. In the aftermath of the 1994 Rwandan genocide, over a million Rwandan Hutu refugees, including members of the Interahamwe militia and the former Rwandan Armed Forces (FAR), fled to Zaire. Many of these groups, along with armed forces from other neighbouring countries, used refugee camps as bases to launch attacks on the new Rwandan government controlled by the Rwandan Patriotic Front (RPF) and led by Paul Kagame. The presence of Hutu génocidaires in eastern Zaire prompted the First Congo War (1996–1997) in which Rwanda and Uganda supported a rebellion against Zairean president Mobutu Sese Seko, backing Laurent-Désiré Kabila's rebel group, the Alliance of Democratic Forces for the Liberation of Congo-Zaire (AFDL). The Congolese government was unable to contain and defeat the opposing forces, leading to the overthrow of Mobutu in May 1997. This marked the beginning of Kabila's rule of the country, whose name he changed back to the Democratic Republic of the Congo.

The Second Congo War, also known as the Great War of Africa, began just over a year later in 1998 and lasted until 2003. During this time numerous rebel groups were active in the DRC, including the Rally for Congolese Democracy (RCD), the Congolese Rally for Democracy-Liberation Movement (RCD-ML) and the Movement for the Liberation of Congo (MLC). The war, which initially erupted when Kabila turned against his former allies from Rwanda, Uganda and Burundi, drew in foreign armies from Zimbabwe, Angola, Namibia and Chad, all of whom came to Kabila's defence against the Rwandan-, Ugandan- and Burundian-aligned militias.

The conflict officially ended on 18 July 2003 in a military stalemate with a fragile peace agreement and a transitional government. From 2003 until late 2024, the DRC experienced relative peace, although numerous rebel groups have taken advantage of the state's incapacity to impose authority. The most notable of these groups is the Rwandan-backed March 23 Movement (known as M23), who have been active in the eastern part of the country since 2012. At their hands, Congolese civilians have been subjected to sexual violence, severe human rights abuses and acute poverty. The struggle for control of lucrative minerals aggravates the situation and contributes to the growth of armed groups. The persistent violence in the east of the DRC is an indication of the enduring challenge of forming effective governance and stability.

Child labour is a serious problem in this region, with rebel groups continuing to exploit young boys and girls. Many child labourers are abducted and forced to work long hours for little or no pay. Children are also forced into sexual slavery and fighting in armed conflicts, or are used as spies and informants. Rebel groups have been known to use children as human shields and suicide bombers.

Child labour not only violates children's rights but also has a devastating effect on the country's economy as a lack of education and skills exacerbates the cycle of poverty. While the DRC government has taken steps to address the issue, a lot more needs to be done to protect the rights of children in the country.

Freedom in the DRC is not just a political aspiration; it is profoundly necessary to break the violence, exploitation and poverty that has plagued the nation for decades. The DRC's history of rebellion and conflict shows the critical importance of establishing true freedom: freedom from oppression, freedom from violence, and freedom to pursue a future filled with hope and opportunity.

In the context of the DRC, building freedom means creating a society where children are not forced into labour or armed conflict but are given the chance to attend school, develop their talents and contribute to the rebuilding of their nation. It means fostering governance structures that prioritise the protection of human rights, the establishment of rule of law and the equitable distribution of the country's vast resources, rather than allowing them to fuel further conflict. Freedom also represents the empowerment of communities to rise above their circumstances, to resist the lure of rebel groups, and to participate in shaping a peaceful and prosperous future. By investing in education, healthcare and economic opportunities, the DRC can begin to heal the wounds of the past and lay the foundation for sustainable peace.

The struggle to build freedom in the DRC is not just a battle against armed groups or corrupt governance; it is a fight for the soul of a nation – a fight to ensure that every Congolese child, woman and man can live with dignity, security and the possibility of a brighter tomorrow. The journey is long and fraught with challenges, but it is a journey that must be undertaken if the DRC is ever to realise its full potential and emerge as a beacon of hope in a region too often defined by conflict and despair.

*

My sister and I belong to the DRC's Bangala tribe based in the northern region close to the equator. Also called *batu yamayi* – people of the water – our people are known for our skill in hunting in water as well as on land.

Because she was educated in Kinshasa, my sister speaks French alongside many local dialects.

In our village, which was close to the town of Zongo, we spoke Lingala.

Yaya means big sister.

Popi means doll.

～

Life started and ended in the village. I never imagined there was a different world somewhere, or people in the world who looked different from me. What I knew was that when it was nighttime in the village, the whole world was sleeping; when it was raining, the whole world was feeling the rain.

That is where I come from.

I was five years old when rebels attacked my village.

2000–2005

Sud-Ubangi province,
Democratic Republic of the Congo

1

I took a deep breath. This time I was determined to get an answer from my sister.

"Why do we live here in the village and not with Mama and Papa, *yaya*?"

*Ya*Ziana lifted her head and looked straight at me, narrowing her brown eyes as if weighing up my readiness for the truth.

"Alright, you've asked so many times. I'll tell you." Her voice was serious. "But this is a difficult story, Popina, so don't interrupt me."

I nodded. I wanted to know.

"I grew up in our family home in a big city called Kinshasa, with our mama and papa, one younger sister and two brothers. Our family had money, and I went to a good school. But something happened to me that I don't want to happen to you. And that's why I will tell you this story.

"One day, when I was ten years old, I was home alone. Papa was on a business trip and Mama was at the market. Our sister Bambino was spending time with her friends and the boys were out as well. I had stayed home to cook and clean – I was cooking *madesu* for the first time, all by myself, and I couldn't wait to share it with Mama once she got home."

I had barely known our mother's cooking, but *Ya*Ziana often talked about the heavenly aromas of Mama's *ndakala*, *pondu* and *fufu* that had filled the house when she was growing up.

"I heard a man's voice asking if anyone was home. It sounded like Papa, so I was surprised to see our Uncle Yendembe in the living room. I went to greet him, and when he kissed me on the cheek I could smell alcohol. He wanted to know where everyone was, and I told him they were out. When I told him that I was cooking, he was very impressed and asked whether I wasn't too young to cook."

*Ya*Ziana went quiet for a moment, looking pensive. Something scurried

5

past the entrance of our hut. We were so used to the small animals from the forest sharing the village with us, we barely took notice.

"You know, Mama once told me she had started cooking at about the same age," she said. "Anyway, Uncle Yendembe said he wanted to show me something but I must close the door first. Then he told me to take off my clothes. I just stood there, not knowing what to do. I thought I must have heard wrong."

Even though I was only five years old, I could sense the darkness in my sister's story. I wrapped my arms around my body, as if to protect myself from what I was about to hear.

"The next thing I knew, he had thrown me on the couch. I couldn't understand why he was so angry with me. His hands were on my neck, his thick fingers squeezing. And he shouted to me that he'd told me to take off my clothes. He slid his hands down my body and told me he'd kill me if I screamed. I was terrified. He took off his belt and … the pain was sudden and intense. My eyes jumped wide open, imprinting his face on my memory. I'll never forget the look in his eyes. It was an expression of triumph, of power, of domination."

At this point, my sister's own face was filled with torment, distorting her delicate features.

"When it was over, he told me this was what uncles did to nieces so that they could become good women. He said there was no shame in it, but it was a secret. If I told Mama or Papa, they would shout at me. Then he got up, got dressed and left me to clean the blood off the couch."

"Did you tell Mama?" I asked cautiously.

"I did. But Uncle Yendembe told Mama and Papa that I had forced myself on him! That it was all my fault! Mama didn't have the courage to stand up for me. Papa didn't have the heart to do the honourable thing either. Instead, everyone went on with their lives as if nothing had happened. And no one protected me."

She paused again.

"But he didn't stop. When I was sixteen years old, they sent me away, to our mama's village, to grow vegetables and raise you." *YáZiana* looked me straight in the eyes. "You see, Popina? That is what it means to be a woman in this world."

She lifted my chin with her finger.

"Now look at me. If anyone ever touches you, I want you to scream as loud as you possibly can. And you must never be afraid to tell me. I'm your sister, your mother, your friend. I will always fight for you. So, there it is, *mwana popi*. I have nothing more to say." She got up and started spreading out our blankets on the floor. "It's late now and we need to wake up at dawn tomorrow."

She blew out the last candle.

"Sleep well, my *popi*."

2

The sun wasn't even up yet when a noise like thunder rattled through our village. The celebratory sound of drums.

"Popina, wake up!" *Ya*Ziana shouted from outside the hut.

I folded up my blanket as best I could, placed it next to *Ya*Ziana's, and got dressed. As I pushed aside the fabric that served as our door, I saw that she was standing next to an enormous wooden mortar, bigger and taller than me.

Even in the dim early morning, my sister was beautiful. I knew that, and so did everybody else. And today she was dressed in a traditional *liputa* wrap with a bright yellow-and-orange floral print. Holding on tightly to a pestle almost the size of a tree trunk, she pounded up and down, crushing dried cassava roots into flour.

Tonight was the hunters' feast – a tradition thousands of years old, a celebration of bravery and courage. It starts with the men going deep into the forest to hunt for food while the women of the village gather to prepare a feast for their return.

A whistle went off in the distance, and I could hear the women's *loi-loi*.

"I've warmed water on the fire for you and Lola," said *Ya*Ziana. "When Lola gets here you can both go take a bath."

And here was my friend running towards me. Two years older than me, Lola had dark skin, wild black hair, a face that was almost perfectly round, and big brown eyes. When she stretched out her arms to hug me, her hair smelt of coconut oil.

"Do you want to climb our tree, Popina?"

That was something else about Lola: she knew the best games.

Sometimes we would watch the bigger girls play *ukugenda*, a game that involves placing stones in a circle or a square drawn in the sand. Each player tries to grab as many stones as they can by throwing one stone in the air and removing the rest of the stones from the circle with their other hand. The person left holding the most stones wins. With my five-year-old hands, I wasn't very good at it yet, but I loved this game.

Or we would watch the boys play soccer. They played in the dust with a cheap plastic ball and bare feet, and when the game was finished they'd all jump in the river to wash. Despite the poverty of our village, a game of soccer was always a happy event – even for the adults.

But as children our greatest pleasure was being free in the wilderness. We would play racing games, or spend hours chatting high up in the forest canopy. We might see a leopard sleeping in a tree or a cave, or baby gorillas running through the forest. Rock rabbits were my favourite. One girl, Benedict, had a rock rabbit pet. Lola and I loved playing with him and watching him follow Benedict around.

The day was calling so I grabbed two *kwanga* dough balls from one of the pots on the floor and tied them to my waist using the fabric of my skirt.

Lola was waiting and we were about to make a run for the forest when *Ya*Ziana said: "Where are you two going without taking a bath?"

Lola turned her bright eyes to my sister. "We'll bath as soon as we get back."

I nodded along eagerly.

"You won't cause any trouble?"

"We promise!" we replied, and off we went, running on our small bare feet.

To get to the forest, we had to pass the hut with the crisp white paint where Mafuta lived. Mafuta was a few years older than us, maybe ten or eleven, and we didn't like him. His father was Papa Liwanga, one of the village decision-makers and a much respected and feared elder. Mafuta's mother was from Nigeria. He had inherited her light skin and hazel eyes, but his pointy chin came from his father, along with his reputation for being a bully. Every child in the village knew about Mafuta's *likonga* – a wooden, Y-shaped slingshot with two rubber strips attached to the uprights. Surrounded by his friends, Mafuta strolled the streets like the king of the land – and if you forgot to obey him, his slingshot would remind you. I'd once seen him shoot a bird nesting in a tree. The nest had fallen to the ground, the fragile eggs smashed to pieces.

Beyond his hut was the land where *Ya*Ziana and I grew tomatoes, yams, beans, bananas, plantains and cassava for our family in the city. Further down the road was the hut where Lola had been born, and which had become my second home. Lola's mother, Mama Nzembo, treated me like I was her own, which helped fill the void left by my own mother.

I never really talked about my mother, but I would lie awake at night thinking about her. *Ya*Ziana had told me that my father was a wealthy man. He owned a farm with plenty of livestock and vegetables, as well as four houses in Kinshasa. One of them had been built especially for my mother – a grand double-storey with large windows and a driveway lined on both sides with mango trees. My father had three other wives, which was acceptable in our culture, and he had been our mother's second husband. Mama's first husband, whom she married at the age of thirteen, had already had five wives. When he had died, his wives and livestock had been passed on to his next brother in line, as was the custom.

Our round hut, I knew, was nothing like Mama's city house, with its giant windows and king-sized beds. Our hut was small and simple, made from mud, logs and grass, with nothing but a black cloth for a door. I wondered what my mother looked like and where she was, and I often dreamt about her. Did she ache for me? When Lola cried, I was jealous seeing Mama Nzembo comfort her.

I still wasn't exactly sure why I had been sent to this village under the care of my sister. In 1996, when I was a baby and she was sixteen, *Ya*Ziana had had to interrupt her education and we'd been sent to the village that my mother had come from, and where she still had land. From then on, my sister had been my only family. She loved me and took care of me, and I knew she would always protect me.

So it seemed to me that I had two mothers in the village: Mama Nzembo and *Ya*Ziana.

*

But this morning as I skipped behind Lola towards the forest, I wasn't thinking about mothers. I was trying to work out how to make my bright top and short gathered skirt look more like Lola's hijab. It was a mystery to me how she could play and climb trees with her long dress covering her whole body except for her face, hands and feet.

Lola wore such a strange dress because of her family's religion – a fact that frightened some people in the village. The real problem for us were the children who chased and mocked Lola. They called her witch, daughter of the black magician. Mafuta's family had started calling her *kindoki* – one possessed by evil spirits. Scary stories circulated through the village about Lola's father's holy book, and how with a flash of a blade he would cut the head off anyone who dared violate it.

*Ya*Ziana had explained to me that Lola's family were Muslims, the only Muslim people in our village. The rest of us believed in the river god, Nisodin, mother of fertility, love, beauty and all creatures. We believed that Mama Nisodin had sacrificed herself so that the world could get a second chance to live, love and grow. *Ya*Ziana herself was a little cautious about Lola's family.

I still remember the first time I heard about the Quran, the forbidden holy book Lola's father had brought with him from the city. *Ya*Ziana had sent me to water our vegetables and as I'd walked past Mafuta's hut I'd heard his parents talking. They'd said that when he'd returned from the city, Lola's father had tried to convince the other villagers to worship his god. Papa Liwanga had said he wouldn't allow it. Lola's father had been forced to leave the village some time ago now, but he'd begged for his wife and daughter to stay in the village until he'd found another home for them.

Mama Nzembo was teaching Lola to read the holy book, but whenever I tried to join in she would stop me and say I wasn't allowed. So I would steal glimpses while they sat reading on the floor. Hands folded in my lap, I'd try to figure out what they were saying and how they knew what was written on the paper pages. I convinced myself that they must be magicians or sorcerers, but I wasn't scared – all I wanted was to be taught the things in the book that I didn't know.

Lola said that God had revealed the message in the book to the final prophet, Muhammad, and that it was about people loving one another and caring for each other.

"But that's also what Mama Nisodin says, so can't they be the same god?" I asked.

She said her mother hadn't told her about that yet, but she was sure she would find out when she was older.

Maybe both our gods will explain this one day, I had thought to myself.

Books were another mystery because there was no school in our village. Our schooling consisted of lessons from the forest and from elders like Papa Franck, who shared stories and wisdom about nature and the spirits.

*

Now Lola turned and looked at me with a smile. It was an effort keeping up with her longer legs and bigger steps, but I ran to catch up with her and took her hand.

There was something else that made Lola special: she always seemed peaceful and happy, immune to insults and incapable of hurting anyone. She never retaliated against her tormentors.

We crossed a river that curved gently through the trees. The forest-filtered light created a constellation of stars on the water.

Lola bent down to splash her face. So did I. It was cool and refreshing, the river making happy bubbling sounds as it slid over rocks. *YaZiana* always told me, "Rivers are the roads of the forest. The first thing a hunter does when he is lost is look for the nearest river."

We continued on our way, but moments later, two mango pits struck Lola in the back.

My heart sank as I turned and saw Mafuta and two of his friends, Kuyonge and Santu. Of all the children who taunted Lola, Mafuta was by far the most relentless. And now he was walking towards us, hands on hips in his colourful shorts and no shirt, casually kicking up stones.

"Good morning, witches!" he exclaimed. "Or should I say *bakindumba*?" Bitches – another of his favourite insults.

Lola stepped in front of me as the three older boys closed in, towering over us. Grinning, Mafuta crossed his thick arms over his chest.

He tipped his chin to me. "Hey, flat nose."

Mafuta and I shared the same beliefs, so he never harassed me the way he harassed Lola. I stayed quiet and crept further behind my friend.

"Have you heard the news?" Mafuta asked. "Anyone who doesn't believe in Mama Nisodin will be kicked out of the village. It's the new rule!"

"That's old news, Mafuta," I replied courageously from behind Lola's back.

"That's old news, Mafuta," he mimicked.

Kuyonge and Santu cackled. I wished *Ya*Ziana was here.

"The new chief, Papa Vanti, ate at our hut. Did you know that too, Popina? And do you know what I'll tell Papa Vanti next time he visits?" Mafuta continued. "I'll talk with him *mungala* to *mungala*, man to man, and tell him that my father says Muslims are crazy. They kill innocent people. They are possessed by demons! Muslims and outsiders must be killed or kicked out of this village!"

"Your mother is an outsider," I said, and then wished I hadn't. And then I wished even harder that *Ya*Ziana was here. Would anyone hear us scream in the forest?

Mafuta ignored me. "My mother says President Kabila is a crazy man, not a great leader. He has killed a lot of innocent people in this country. If he had never become president, DRC would be better now. Do you little girls know the difference between a country and a village?"

I shook my head. I didn't know, but Mafuta always answered his own questions anyway. His hazel eyes flicked towards Lola.

"Where we live is called a village, and a village is in a country," he explained with mock authority. "And our village is for true spiritual seekers. We are the people of water, the true Bangalas, not this *kindoki* here. When we die, we become part of the soil, the trees and the air, but your people pollute our homeland and our souls. You dirty our country."

Mafuta's friends moved closer.

"Mafuta, you must ask the new chief to get rid of the Muslim people," said Santu.

"Just let us go!" With a trembling voice Lola finally broke her silence. "We're not bothering you."

"You *are* bothering me," Mafuta said. "You bother me more than baboons and monkeys." Mafuta shifted his gaze to me. "How can you talk to her, play with her, eat her mother's food?" he said with disgust.

His friends grunted in agreement. With a sinking heart I saw Kuyonge reach for something from his back pocket. Another slingshot, red and brand new.

"How can you call her your friend?" Santu added.

Mafuta gave me a warning look. "You're the problem, Popina. You and your sister. If idiots like you didn't talk to them, eat with them, we wouldn't have such people here, people who believe they can pray to whoever they want. You're a disgrace to our people and our village."

I could see that he wanted to hurt us. He raised his slingshot and aimed it at me.

"Girls are weak and stupid. What are you doing here in the forest anyway? Shouldn't you be cooking and cleaning?"

Santu nodded. "Yes, the forest is for men only."

I think Lola must have had enough because that's when she kicked Mafuta in the chest. He toppled off his feet and his eyes widened as he fell to the ground – Lola was strong for her size.

She grabbed my hand and off we ran. "Leave us alone!" she shouted over her shoulder.

Behind us Mafuta shouted: "This doesn't end today, little girl. And it's not the end for you either, Popina."

Walking home to the village, Lola and I didn't say much but we stayed alert, ready to run like horses if Mafuta and his friends ambushed us. They didn't, but that didn't make us feel any better.

3

Drumming welcomed us back. In the village streets, the hunters' feast had already started. And there were the proud young men, skin shiny with coconut oil, muscles bulging, loincloths around their waists. They rubbed the sides of their heads against each other in a special greeting; it was forbidden for women to greet this way.

Masked dancers sang and danced to the rhythm of the drums, their bodies painted red to symbolise how all of creation is connected through blood – that the blood that flows through an animal's veins is the same as that which flows through ours. We all have different vessels that carry our souls, but we share a life on earth. *Ya*Ziana had told me that's why it was important during the hunt to thank the animals for the life they lived and for their sacrifice.

Whispering and giggling in each other's ears, the young women watched the hunters as they danced alongside the masked dancers. Older mamas, dressed up in their finest prints and *kitambalas*, sat in a row opposite the papas, singing and clapping along to the music, while the older men poured *cham-cham* on the ground, respectfully sharing their drinks with the ancestors so that they too could celebrate and protect the people.

And there was *Ya*Ziana and four other women playing their part in the display, walking in a straight line towards us, carrying on their heads the clay pots they had made. They wore short skirts and tops that wrapped across their breasts, the colourful prints bold in the bright sunlight. Their faces and arms were painted, and they wore special beads around their necks, hands and feet.

As two mamas walked past with buckets of plantain, they exclaimed over the beautiful pottery – and I wanted to burst because I knew I had the most beautiful and hardworking sister in the village.

As young as I was, I already knew the importance of pottery for women.

Clay pots were used to prepare and cook food, and to store water, but the elders also believed that pottery could teach a young woman important life lessons. Pottery requires balance: if you lean too much one way, your pot will be lopsided and break. Shaping pots requires patience: if you rush, it won't turn out the way you want it to.

If I had been older then, I might also have understood what clay teaches about change: that nothing stays the same and change is part of life, even if it isn't easy. Clay goes from being soft, wet and waxy, to chalky and delicate as it dries, to strong and sturdy after firing. A pot must go through each of these different stages. It's the same with women, my people were taught. We look, feel and express ourselves differently in every stage of life. The transition between stages might be tough – we endure pressure from shaping and heat – but the elders say this is necessary, and worth it.

Grabbing Lola's hand, I ran towards *Ya*Ziana, but just then one of the elders blew a whistle and the drumming, singing and dancing intensified, making it difficult for me to reach her. People started clapping their hands – "*Yelele*," they ululated. "*Wacha, yelele*!" they cheered.

With raised arms, the women moved in circles. One woman – eyes darkened with charcoal below a pink-and-green *kitambala*, cheeks glistening and face round like the moon – reached out to us and gracefully spun us around by our wrists. Bells strapped around her ankles jingled as she moved to the rhythm and there I was dancing, clapping, singing with Lola. With her feet, the woman pounded the ground to the beat and sang, "*Yelele! Bina*, dance!"

Soon *Ya*Ziana and her friends were *loi-loing* and laughing right beside us, shaking their hips and tilting their heads back and forth.

Eventually nighttime came and the whole village gathered around a huge fire to listen to stories told by the elders and healers.

"Bring the children to the fire!" called Papa Franck. Thin as a reed, Papa Franck had deep-set eyes and a nose with wide, flaring nostrils, and he was much loved by us children. "I will share a special story tonight."

He lifted his pipe to his lips and inhaled deeply, then exhaled through his nose. The smoke drifted away in thin grey threads.

I sat next to Lola, curling my legs beneath me, my hands pressed against the cooling soles of my feet. We waited for the story and for the peanuts *Ya*Ziana was toasting for us over the flames. I breathed in the fresh evening air drifting from the forest. The sky was a blanket of stars, flashing and flickering as if feasting with us.

Finally, when everyone was settled around the fire, Papa Franck stood up to tell his story.

*

Once upon a time, he started, in the days when spirits and gods roamed the land, there lived a little girl with dark-brown eyes named Nisodin. She charmed everyone with her energy, overflowing kindness and good heart. She was an only child, living with her family in a little village called Zongo.

Life in Zongo was hard. In the valleys to the west there were trees with juicy fruits and flowers, and streams with cold, clear water. But Zongo was a desolate place cursed by the gods. There had been a drought for many years and finding water was a daily struggle because the village wells, even the deep ones, often ran low. The villagers had to walk for half a day to reach the nearest river, and its waters flowed muddy all year.

After twenty years of drought, most of the animals and trees had died and the river had dried up. But Nisodin and her family considered themselves fortunate and cherished life above all things. Nisodin would often visit the big dry river and would roam around the forest talking to the dead trees and plants. She was sure that they were still alive and that the *mbula munene*, the heavy rain, was coming.

One day, when Nisodin was at the river, she saw a green-blue light floating in the air. She followed the light to a place in the desert where there had once been a lush forest with lakes and wild animals. The light suddenly stopped moving, but when Nisodin tried to touch it, it slipped out of her hands and rotated around her.

A fallen star, she thought, mesmerised – she had never seen anything like it before. So when it started moving again she followed it, walking many hours until the sun was just a faint red glow in the distance.

Nisodin was so eager to touch the star that she followed it through valleys and mountains, all the way to the top of *Kongenge Mabangu* – Shining Mountain.

*

"That's where the mountain got its name." Papa Franck took a drag from his pipe and poked at the fire with a stick. Small sparks scattered before disappearing into the night.

I shifted to straighten my legs.

Beside me, Lola stared past Papa Franck into the darkness.

*

Then Nisodin tried to grab at the light, and when she did, it stopped, came straight towards her face and entered her mouth. And as soon as the light entered Nisodin's mouth, she fell into a deep sleep. She slept for three days on the mountain.

On the first day, when Nisodin's mother had seen that the sun was getting low as the hills, she'd begun to wonder where her daughter was. She'd gone from hut to hut asking if anyone had seen her precious *mwana popi*, her baby doll. And every day after that the neighbours had searched for her.

Three days passed and still no one could find Nisodin. At the same time, life in the village was becoming unbearable. Several babies died of thirst in their banana-leaf cradles and the wells ran ever lower. Nisodin's mother and father kept praying to the gods to help them find their daughter. They hardly ate and just sat inside the hut alone, two figures gazing through the doorway. The people of the village started thinking that no one would ever see the poor child again, and a rumour began circulating that she'd been eaten by animals.

But after three days on the mountain, Nisodin awoke from her sleep.

Her feet were bloodied from the long walk and her hair was caked with desert dust, but she started walking back home, even though the wind nearly tore her from the side of the mountain.

In the village of Zongo, Nisodin's parents were sitting in the dirt at the edge of the family field, scanning the horizon. With prayers on their lips and hope in their hearts they suddenly saw a small figure approaching from the direction of the mountains. She was very thin and wearing threadbare rags, and at first they thought it was one of the village's younger girls. It wasn't until she came closer that they recognised their daughter, Nisodin. Seeing her sunken eyes, their hearts leapt with joy, and they cried with relief.

After she had washed and had some water to drink and food to eat, Nisodin and her family gathered around the fire with the other villagers, who peppered her with questions.

"Where did you go, Nisodin?"

"What did you see?"

"What happened to you?"

Nisodin couldn't say anything because the answers were beyond anyone's imaginings. She remembered the light she'd seen, how she'd followed it to the mountains, how it had entered her mouth. In her deep sleep she had ended up in another world. And now it was as though she had woken from a beautiful dream.

"How long have I been away?" she asked.

"Three days," said the villagers.

Nisodin gasped. "Three days only? It felt much longer."

But Nisodin fell ill and she died seven days later. As she was dying there was great rainfall – not soft drizzle that evaporates before it even touches the ground. No, sheets of water poured from the sky, meeting the thirsty village. All week the water drummed upon the roofs of the huts of Zongo, drowning out all other sounds. The wells filled and the river rose. The hills in the east turned green as wildflowers bloomed. For the first time in many years, children played in the trees again and the hunters started hunting. Everyone rejoiced.

When the rain stopped, the villagers had work to do. Several mud walls had been washed away, a few of the roofs were sagging and entire fields had been turned into forest swamps. But the people of Zongo didn't complain. Instead, new walls were erected, roofs repaired and more huts built. The villagers produced the most plentiful plantain and cassava crops of their lives, and the size and quality of the crops increased more in the next year, and the next, and the next.

And no drought ever came to Zongo again.

*

Papa Franck paused and looked at the crowd around him, shifting his gaze from one face to the next as if making sure the story had seeped right into our souls.

The only sound was the crackling of the fire.

After what felt like an eternity, he broke the silence.

"There's so much to say about the small girl who sacrificed her life for our village and its people. Whenever we go to the river to fetch water, of which there is now plenty, we should give thanks to Nisodin for the bounty she has brought us."

I gazed up at the sky. A few wispy clouds floated past the moon and I sighed as a soft wind curled down from the mountains, disturbing the fire.

"That's the end for today," said Papa Franck. "Rain is coming."

YaZiana stretched out her arms and pulled me close. I could smell spice on her clothes from the food she'd been cooking all day.

She leant over me and whispered into my ear: "To want more than this, to wish for more, is bad for the mind and the heart."

I rested my head against the curve of her neck. I didn't wish for anything more. If ever I was content in my life, this was the moment.

When I think back, the bliss and simplicity seem almost surreal. If only I had realised then how lucky I was, how happy. And how innocent life could be.

4

*Ya*Ziana always woke when the first cock crowed and the shrill calls of the night crickets were fading. Outside she would start making a fire to boil water for us to drink and then wash in, and then she would wake me up.

The morning after the hunters' feast was no different. The light inside the hut was dim as the crowing of a rooster drifted through the doorway.

"Popina" – *Ya*Ziana gently patted my shoulder – "wake up. We must go fetch water."

I tried to pry open my stinging eyes. The villagers had celebrated deep into the night, and I had barely slept. But the sweet smell of warm coconut milk – our breakfast – filled the hut, so I tied my wrap over my vest and leggings and folded up my sleeping blanket.

*Ya*Ziana started telling me about a dream she'd had.

"I'm not sure where exactly I was. It was warm and sunny, and I remember seeing a lot of people clapping hands," she said. "Who they were clapping for, I couldn't see."

She poured me a cup of coconut milk and I blew on the hot liquid, watching the steam make softly curling patterns in the air.

"What does it mean?" I asked.

"I don't know. I was hoping you could tell me." *Ya*Ziana started peeling a plantain. She put it on a plate and handed it to me.

"Well, *I* don't know." I giggled. "But Mama Nzembo says dreams always mean something."

But *Ya*Ziana seemed suddenly cross. "Popina! Mama Nzembo spends too much time reading books and talking to herself. She doesn't look men in the eye and she doesn't always return a greeting. Be careful around her. And don't take what she says too seriously."

I took a sip of my coconut milk. "But she knows *everything, yaya*. Maybe she can read you something from her book."

*Ya*Ziana waved her hand. "Come on, drink up. We need to fetch water for the house and water the vegetables. If you want, I'll plait your hair after lunch."

Once we had finished our breakfast, *Ya*Ziana picked up our water container, which was almost big enough for me to climb into.

"You can carry it while it's empty," she said, handing it to me.

She picked up our black bucket and we started walking.

Down the road, Mama Nzembo and Lola were facing away from us, north of the rising sun. They were kneeling on beautiful rugs, one each, and they bent down to kiss the ground, their hands placed gently next to their faces. I could see Mama Nzembo's feet, a golden bracelet sparkling on her right ankle.

"O Allah, I ask You for well-being in this world and the Hereafter," said Mama Nzembo aloud. "O Allah, I ask You for pardon and well-being in my religion, my worldly affairs, my family and my property. O Allah, conceal my faults and keep me safe from what I fear."

It looked to me like they were talking to their rugs, but in a quiet voice *Ya*Ziana explained that they were talking to their god.

"O Allah, guard me from in front of me and behind me, on my right and on my left, and from above me."

Another group of women walked past them and started to laugh. I wondered why Lola and her mother had to talk to their god outside. The villagers wouldn't make fun of them if they at least stayed inside their hut.

"O Allah, bless my husband, Muhammad. Let the sun not set on his prosperity, inshallah. Lift the curse they have put on him. Bless my daughter, Lola. Give her enough and bless her future."

A bird called from close by, drawn-out and plaintive. Mama Nzembo's voice was calm as the forest on a windless day.

"O Allah, bless Ziana and her little sister, Popina. Guide them away from evil and towards good, inshallah."

I was surprised that Mama Nzembo was praying for us with the same earnestness that she had prayed for her own family.

"And I seek refuge in Your Magnificence from being swallowed up from beneath me."

Lola was moving her hands up and down. I wished she would turn and see me, but she was absorbed in her prayer, and we passed quietly by.

*

*Ya*Ziana said that the forest wasn't safe, and she always insisted that I walk beside her instead of running ahead. There were a lot of snakes, she said, and I had to watch where I stepped.

In the forest the grass was soft beneath our feet, thick from the recent rain. The trees stood their ground proudly as kings, their knobbly arms rising to the heavens, further than my eyes could see. An orchestra of birdsong played around us.

But the daily journey to fetch water wasn't easy. It was a long way to the river, thorns littered the path and we had to walk back carrying heavy containers. It was even more tiring when it was hot, which it almost always was. But *Ya*Ziana and I shared many laughs as we went, and it was also a time to ask her more serious things.

Today I asked why I had never seen Mafuta or the other boys fetching water.

Holding the empty bucket in front of her, back straight, eyes turned upwards, my sister looked as if she was searching for something.

"Because it's a *woman's* job," she replied after some time, and she made it sound like a very important job. That made me feel important too – the same way I felt when she smiled at me.

At the river there were many other women – mothers with small children on their backs, some pregnant, all scooping water into the large containers they would be carrying back home, containers that could weigh as much as a child. One elderly woman, her face enmeshed with fine lines, looked too old to be carrying water by herself. Some women helped her balance the heavy canister on her head as she gripped her loose *liputa* to her bony waist.

Just then, *YaZiana's* friend Sanza joined us. She was wearing a short colourful dress that emphasised her curves, a brown *kitambala* wrapped around her head. She carried an empty container in one hand and swatted at a buzzing fly with the other. Sanza often came to visit our hut at lunchtime. She liked to sit and gossip about other people and their business.

"Good morning, Ziana! *Oza ndenge nini?* How's it going?" she greeted.

"We're well," replied *YaZiana*. "Our buckets are almost full – get your water quickly so we can go."

Soon we were walking back to the village, me carrying the smaller black bucket as the full container was now too heavy.

"Popina," said Sanza, "walk in front so we grown-ups can talk."

I can't wait until I'm old enough to listen, I thought as I walked ahead of them – but not so far that I couldn't eavesdrop.

"Did you see Niala's big stomach?" Sanza was saying. "People are talking! This girl has not only brought shame to her family but has reduced her own worth. What man is going to want to marry a woman who opened her womb before marriage? They are suspecting Elder Pathi to be the father of the child."

"Well, is he?"

"Why would I lie to you, Ziana? Elder Pathi, of course, denies it. So now her breasts will go soft for a man who's rejected her in front of the whole village! Such a shame."

I looked up, allowing the ever-changing light and shadows to dance across my face. A chorus of birdsong filled the air and I breathed in the sweet smell of forest flowers.

"Popina, look!" *YaZiana* called out. "Quickly, before it disappears – *mbulu*, an African peafowl!"

This was a bird I had never seen before. With its bright feathers, a metallic-green shimmering in the sun, I'd never seen anything more beautiful.

"Now close your eyes and tell it what you want. It'll bring good luck," my sister added. "We are very lucky to see it."

But I couldn't close my eyes. The bird started running away, but then it stopped and it seemed to look back at me.

"Popina, you have to close your eyes!" *YaZiana* shouted.

I realised I was holding my breath. Slowly, I exhaled. But I felt paralysed – like I had glimpsed something magical. Like my spirit had connected with the bird.

"Come on, Popina!" Sanza shouted, breaking my trance. "Ziana, tell her to carry on walking."

*

It was midday when we got back home. My sister started to prepare *fufu* with thick chunks of boiled mutton and dark-green cassava leaves.

"Stay and eat with us, Sanza." *YaZiana* gestured at the mat. After just a moment's hesitation, Sanza sat.

We ate in silence. With my fingers I moulded my *fufu* into small balls and dipped it in the mutton soup, making sure to scoop up the soft meaty chunks.

"You're so big now, Popina," Sanza teased. "Soon, the suitors will start coming!"

I looked at her confused, because all I could think about was the peafowl and the feeling I'd had when our eyes had locked. Sanza moved her attention back to *YaZiana* and they carried on talking about the village boys.

After we'd eaten, *YaZiana* fetched the comb. I think she enjoyed plaiting my hair more than I did. It took ages to braid because my hair was thick, and it would spring back into a dense bunch as soon as the comb had passed through it. I would pretend my scalp was itchy as an excuse to reach up and feel how far she still had to go – and it took the rest of the afternoon.

I was five years old, and that was the last day I felt like a child.

It was also the last time I would experience peace in my village.

5

Lola and I hopped over the stick fence that surrounded the wild mango trees. We had spent the next morning climbing their branches, eating too many sour mangoes and chasing the baby baboons that had strayed from their troops. With juice still dripping down our faces, we'd picked the sweetest mangoes to bring home with us, and now we ran back across an open field that was littered with old paper, plastic and clothes – discarded things that were slowly becoming one with the soil. It was a long way home, and it would soon be midday.

A group of men we didn't recognise were sitting huddled together nearby, smoking. But we weren't scared – they were just a group of people, and the men in our village were not violent. The only crime we knew was when someone stole a piece of fabric or someone else's fruit. We had no reason to be wary.

One of them spotted us. He elbowed the guy next to him and called out to us.

"Hey, you!" he said. "I know you."

He was a tall man with a shaved head and a black beard. Neither Lola nor I had ever seen him before.

"I think just keep walking," Lola muttered under her breath.

"You! The Muslim! Look at me when I'm talking to you!" the tall man yelled. He handed his smoke to his friend and pointed the middle finger of his other hand up at the sky, moving it up and down, up and down. I had no idea what he was pointing at.

"I knew your mother, did you know that? I took her from behind by that creek over there." The men laughed, and one of them made a squealing sound.

Now we understood that these men were not friendly. Lola put a protective arm around my shoulders and told me to keep on walking.

"We ate her really well," he said, grinning and shaking hands with the others. Then he started walking towards us.

"*Yaka to kima* – let's run!" Lola shouted.

I dropped the mangoes I was carrying, and we started running on our baby legs. But I tripped over a stone, and the men were around us before I could even get up.

"Where's your attitude now, little girl?" the tall man said. He had a knife in his right hand. "Didn't you hear me when I called you?"

He stood over me, fists curled, legs slightly apart, staring at me while I tried to get up. I felt every muscle in my body brace, and something cold crept up my spine.

The man kept playing with his knife. The others shifted nervously on their feet, looking from us to the tall man as if they had cornered some wild animals that only their leader could tame.

"Can you speak, little girl?" he asked Lola.

She didn't move.

"Do you know what we do to girls like you?" He let out a loud laugh.

My fear was numbing. I closed my eyes – I couldn't look at his face.

"We have to kill her before they become too many!" one of the men shouted.

The tall man turned to me, pointing the knife at my face. "Are you also Muslim?"

"It's only the one dressed like that," said another man, pointing a gun right in Lola's face. A huge scar ran along his cheek, and he had long hair like a lion's mane.

I kept my face lowered as tears slid down my cheeks.

"Please let us leave," Lola said softly.

But two of the men started shoving her side to side as if playing a game of catch. Then the tall man pushed me down so I fell flat on my back, stones slicing into my skin. He started taking off his pants, and then his erect penis was bobbing over me as I lay there on the ground. He grabbed my legs and forced them apart. I tried to scream, but my mouth was bone dry. All I could manage was a weak croak.

"She's not Muslim, I am!" Lola cried out.

The tall man let go of me, and I wrapped my legs around each other, locking them shut. The man turned back to Lola.

"We need to teach you evil worshippers a lesson," he said. "You need to be punished."

"Yes, and this one is very cheeky," one of the other men added, tearing off Lola's hijab.

The tall man walked over to Lola and slapped her hard across the face. She let out a scream that the air seemed to absorb as it left her throat. He grabbed hold of her, pushed her to the ground and tried to force her legs apart. But she kept on tossing and kicking.

"Open your legs!" he yelled.

He had his full weight on top of her now. He pulled back his hand and slapped her again, even harder than before. The other men stood laughing. With the second slap, Lola gave in.

I'd heard the older people talk about attacks on other villages, how the soldiers mercilessly raped women and young girls like us. I hadn't understood it, and I don't think I would have believed it. Now, with overwhelming numbness, I realised that it wasn't just a story, and we were about to be next.

One of the other men started moving towards me.

I picked up the largest stone I could see. As the man climbed on top of me, I squeezed the stone in my hand. Suddenly, with tremendous strength, I brought the stone to the side of his thigh and hit him. The other men laughed.

I hit him again. He slapped me twice in the face.

As quickly as it came, my strength was gone. His hands were ten times bigger than mine. His body was weighing me down, and I was battling to breathe. I started screaming.

"*Ya*Ziana! *Ya*Ziana! Lola!"

I knew *Ya*Ziana wouldn't hear me. I couldn't even hear myself. Was I making any sound at all?

With force, the man ripped off my clothes. When I looked towards Lola, there was already blood. I felt my thighs cracking open.

I shut my eyes as he entered my body. Never in my life had I felt such pain. It was as if somebody was cutting through my flesh with a blunt knife. I didn't move. I was made of stone. Inside, I cried for my sister to find me so that this could be over.

Around my head, all sound was muted except for a repetitive rasping, over and over again. The man covered my face with one hand so I couldn't see. I couldn't breathe. My legs were dead, the pain between them so intense I wished I would die.

They all took turns with us.

When I dared to look, there was blood everywhere. My blood. My blood pouring down my legs into the soil.

The last man spat on me. He said it was for good luck.

*

When I opened my eyes, the men were gone.

I was still lying on the ground. The sun had made its way across the sky but there was still no shade. The heat beat down. My body was broken. Staring at the blue sky, I realised there weren't any birds. No wing flaps or bird calls. No sounds of nearby people or even monkeys or baboons. The world had gone completely quiet, like everyone we knew had abandoned us.

Who could we run to? Our homes were too far away. And the more I wanted to call for help, the bigger and lonelier the world felt. The only thing I could hear was the sound of my own breathing and my noisy thoughts.

I was so confused.

Was this my fault?

Would my sister find me, find us?

I looked over at Lola and our eyes met. She reached out her hand and slowly we rolled across to one another until we were holding each other tight, shivering in shock.

"What are we going to do?" I asked Lola.

She didn't have an answer.

*

Eventually, we gathered the strength to get up. Our clothes were in shreds and there was nothing to cover our bodies, so we walked home naked.

Little children in the village often played naked, but there was now a feeling of shame. I urgently needed to cover myself before someone tried to hurt me again.

At first, as we entered the village, the mamas scolded us: "Where are your clothes?"

But one woman quickly realised. She put her hands on her head and started screaming.

"They're here to kill our children, oh God!"

"Ziana! Come get your sister!"

Mama Nzembo was there and then I saw *Ya*Ziana and ran straight into her arms. As she held me, more tears started to fall. She took the *liputa* from around her waist and gently covered me before walking me home.

In our hut I told her everything. She listened patiently between my tears.

"Don't cry, I'm here now," she said softly. Her reassurance made me feel that even though a man is never wrong, this wasn't my fault – and that I was brave for telling her.

"When you have eaten, I'll bathe you," she said with sadness in her eyes.

Soon Lola and Mama Nzembo came over. Lola was quiet; she just sat there curled up in her mother's arms, staring blankly ahead.

*Ya*Ziana had already prepared a meal of *fufu* and a thin soup with chunks of meat, fish and boiled white yams. She brought us a bowl of water to wash our hands, and Lola's mother said grace, asking Allah to bless the food.

I didn't have an appetite, but *Ya*Ziana kept telling me that I should try. My tongue felt like paper, my body stiff with shock. In my head I could still hear my own screams, and images of the men flashed before my eyes.

After the meal *Ya*Ziana filled a bucket with water. Normally when she didn't want to make a fire she would put the bucket outside to heat up in the sun and I would bath outside. This time she brought the bucket inside the hut.

It was big enough for my little body to be completely immersed. I sat in the soapy water for a long time, long after *Ya*Ziana had finished washing me.

I was pretending that the water was a shield that could protect me from the world.

*

Neither of us were able to sleep that night. *Ya*Ziana sat by the opening that was our door, a long stick in her hands.

I lay curled tight like a baby on my blanket on the floor. Eventually I closed my eyes – if I let the darkness cover me, maybe there would be no fear.

6

In the morning, I woke to an excruciating burning between my thighs. I tried to stretch, but it was too painful. From outside came the sound of sheep bleating in the distance, the high-pitched whistles of shepherds. I tucked my legs close to my body and wrapped my arms around them. My head pulsed. I felt utterly alone.

I didn't want to leave the safe darkness of our hut. Something told me I needed to hide from the tall man and his comrades. That he was coming back for me, that it wasn't over yet.

Footsteps – someone was walking towards the hut.

I panicked. Where was *YaZiana*?

"Good morning, *popi*."

Instant relief at my sister's voice.

Behind her, through the door opening, I could see Lola and her mother. Mama Nzembo was wearing a green dress with a black shawl wrapped tightly around her face.

"Good morning, Ziana. *Oza ndenge nini?*" Mama Nzembo asked softly as she entered our hut. "I have come to check up on you girls. How are you doing, Popina?"

My mouth couldn't form any words. I felt sick.

Nyota, one of the village girls, called from outside. "Popina! Lola! Come play!" Nyota was funny – her hair was short like a boy's, and she wore only boys' pants because she had eight brothers and her mother said there wasn't money for girls' clothes.

We didn't feel like playing, not this morning, but *YaZiana* insisted that we join the game – she needed to start her daily chores. Mama Nzembo offered to watch us.

I got up from my bed on the floor and stood in the doorway. I could see the girls playing *ukugenda* outside. Over the road from our hut, the boys were playing soccer. I watched as someone kicked their ball into the forest and a boy called Beya ran to fetch it. He was coming out of the bushes when a bullet pierced his head.

I was just standing there in front of our hut.

And I saw Beya die.

And then gunshots shook our hut and suddenly there were soldiers everywhere. *Ya*Ziana, Mama Nzembo, Lola and I, standing there together as soldiers came out of nowhere, running in all directions, stopping and searching people – what for? – firing guns, torching huts.

Everything happened in slow motion. I felt as if I had left my body and was looking at the scene from somewhere else. All around us huts were going up in flames, mothers screaming for their children. I saw a man kneeling, his hands raised in the air. A single bullet in the back.

Soon the ground was littered with bodies, limp and lifeless like cloth dolls, but these were people I knew.

I looked around me, rooted to the spot. Was this really happening? My mind told me to run, but my limbs wouldn't move. My child-brain didn't comprehend this. Couldn't comprehend that Burundian rebels were invading our village. Collecting people. Collecting little girls and boys. Killing the older men and women.

All around me, people were dying. I gazed out over the wasteland that had been our village, our home.

And then a shot rang out, much closer.

Mama Nzembo collapsed. Blood poured out of her mouth as she hit the ground. Lola screamed, then was off like lightning to reach her. She put her hands around her mother's neck.

A sound raw with grief. "Wake up! Wake up, Mama! *Please!*"

A boy in a soldier's uniform tried to grab Lola and pull her away, but she tightened her grip. He struck her, bright-red streams flowed down her face. She kept clinging to her mother but the boy, impatient, tore her away.

My sister was holding me. Now she grabbed Lola. The village was so open – we could run into the forest. But the soldiers were shouting commands to those who were still alive. Anyone who dared to run was shot. I didn't understand their language, but *Ya*Ziana did: we had to line up in two rows, females and males separately.

A white truck idled past our line, spitting a suffocating cloud of dust in our faces. Stern-faced young men and boys sat on their haunches in the back, guns slung casually over their shoulders. Some already had beards, some had bushy hair and some wore red turbans. A young man with thick knitted eyebrows swatted the side of the truck with a whip. When my eyes met his, it felt like my flesh had shrunk against my bones. He looked away and I started breathing again.

"What's the matter with you?" *Ya*Ziana hissed. "Don't stare at them! Keep your eyes on your feet when the soldiers are near you. Do you understand me?"

They handcuffed us and put shackles around our ankles, linking us with chains and padlocks. With wide eyes I glanced over at *Ya*Ziana. Lola was crying.

They commanded us to start walking but the weight of metal made it hard to move.

"We're going to be alright, don't worry," *Ya*Ziana tried to reassure from behind me. "Be very quiet. Don't look anyone in the eyes, Popina. Always keep your head down. Same for you, Lola."

I glanced back at the village. I could feel the heat of the flames on my face – our home being consumed by fire.

The dark-grey smoke shrouded the morning sun.

The world was in flames.

*

So many bodies falling down.

And I am so small.

What are they going to do to us? Will I end up dead too?

This is the end for me.

*

My feet hurt. I was exhausted and hungry. Terrified.

In the afternoon, after walking, chained, for hours along a narrow foot-path, we reached the village of Kumase.

I had never been to Kumase, but the people of my village often travelled there by donkey or horse to trade livestock, seed and crops. The village was known to be very beautiful, a jewel in the crown of the DRC. Its lush rolling hills were shrouded in soft mist and people said it was impossible not to see the hand of the Creator in the green valley and sparkling lakes. They said that the hearts of the Kumase people reflected this beauty – they were known for their kindness and loving nature. Some said the people from Kumase, the Muswahilis, were taller than us, with light skins and narrow noses – our people, the Bangalas, were shorter, darker and broad-nosed. But the two tribes had been marrying each other for centuries. We shared the same history, we had the same culture and we farmed the same land.

To my childish eyes, we were one people.

As we entered the village, the rebels wasted no time – they did what they had done in our village. There was a cacophony of gunshots and shouting, and fires started lighting up everywhere. Soon children's bodies were scattered all over the ground, people screaming while being chained. Were my eyes deceiving me? Was this how people treated other people?

The rebels made us prisoners kneel on the ground and pointed guns at us. No one dared move. I was leaning forward, my head facing down, when I heard a woman cry out close to me. Looking across at her, I could see that she was pregnant. Tears were streaming down her face, and her dress was covered in blood.

"My baby! My baby! My baby!" she was screaming. "Please help me!"

One of the soldiers walked over to her. He raised his gun to her swollen belly. Bang! Bang! Bang! Bang! She fell, and for a moment, her chest kept rising and falling. But then it stopped. Her eyes turned glassy, her arms limp. Four shots, two lives.

Behind the woman was a beautiful teak tree. A young man was tied to the tree trunk with a rope, his face puffy and turning a pale shade of blue, his clothes shredded and bloody.

Next to me, Lola was trembling uncontrollably.

"It's your own people you are killing," a voice said from the line of men next to me. It belonged to an old man, his right cheek bleeding. He barked a wet cough and spat on the ground. Then he looked straight at me. "Keep your eyes on your feet, little girl," he said more quietly.

I started crying. *I am going to die. I am going to die. I am going to die.*

But then a voice whispered in my ear: *Not today, Popina.*

I am going to die – the only thought I had.

You are not, the voice whispered.

I looked around. "*Ya*Ziana," I whispered, "can you hear that voice?"

"What voice?"

*

The rebels captured many more people in Kumase, chaining them up like animals. Finally, we moved on, about eighty captives of men, women and children, leaving behind only smoke, ashes and death. Taking only memories of the lives we used to know.

7

We walked for two days, watching the same thing done to other villages, more people chained to our line. For the rest of the time we walked through the forest in a numb daze, stones and sticks slicing our bare feet. We ate nothing. We slept just as we were.

Eventually, through the trees, the outlines of a camp became visible – the rebels' main base. Dirty-white army tents had been set up in a rough clearing and soldiers in green uniforms guarded access to the forest. Every now and again shouts and whistles penetrated the silence.

I blinked in shock. It was not my imagination – dead bodies were dangling from the trees.

The soldiers ordered us into the camp. They were in good spirits, clapping hands and singing, and soon, like hungry animals, feasting on mangoes and nuts. Some walked right up to us and pushed their rifles into our faces, mocking us. They harassed the females, telling us to take off our clothes, sometimes ripping off a dress without warning.

In the scorching sun, my thirst, hunger and exhaustion were now overwhelming.

A group of young boys stood to the side smoking cigarettes. One of them waved his gun in the air as if to remind us that our lives were now in their hands. In the line alongside ours, I saw Mafuta. He was staring at the ground, avoiding eye contact with the soldiers. His face was bruised and one eye was swollen shut, his lower lip puffed up and discoloured.

"Mafuta!" From our line, Mafuta's mother had caught sight of her son.

He nodded at her, tear stains on his face. His father was nowhere to be seen – maybe powerful Papa Liwanga had been killed in the village.

Next to her, a woman was pleading with one of the soldiers. She spoke in low tones at first, but then her voice raised to a shrill cry. "Can't you see he's just a little boy? He's only eight years old! How will he carry a gun?"

She was pointing at Djamba, one of the boys I played with in the village. He had a lost look about him, his eyes full of fear. Why, I wondered, would Djamba need a gun?

As we stood waiting on the edge of the camp, a three-legged dog emerged from the forest behind us. He was scrawny, with a wiry tail and flea-ridden ears. He took a few steps in our direction but then sniffed, turned and limped back into the forest.

I watched him go with inconsolable sadness.

I wished I was him.

And I wonder now, if I had known that this captivity would last for five long years, if I should have risked running after him.

*

The man who appeared to be in charge shot into the air. We would later find out that his name was Kantu wa Milandu, but we would call him Three Eyes because he wore an eye patch. Like some of the rebels, he could speak our language. Most of the others, we would learn, spoke Swahili.

"Get ready to move!" Three Eyes shouted in Lingala.

His second-in-command pointed a gun at us. "Anybody run, I shoot."

"Now move!" Three Eyes shouted again.

They directed us to some open ground and told us to stand facing each other – the line of women and girls on one side, the men and boys on the other.

"Unchain the men," Three Eyes ordered.

As they did, a boy broke away from the line and started running. Three Eyes' right-hand man pointed his gun and shot the boy in the head. His brains splayed all over the ground.

The soldier pointed his gun back at us. "I'll say it again: if you run, we shoot." Then to the men and boys: "Take off your clothes!"

No one moved.

"Are you all deaf? Do you want me to shoot every single one of you? Take off your clothes!"

Slowly, the men and boys started taking off their clothes. Feeling sick with hunger and fear, I looked down and closed my eyes.

"You with the green dress, look up!" a soldier shouted. He walked up to me, lifted my chin with his rough hands, and looked straight into my eyes.

"Unchain all the women and girls!" Three Eyes commanded. "And take off their clothes!"

A woman started screaming and crying: "Please! I'm begging you! Leave my baby girl!"

I noticed that not all the soldiers seemed comfortable with what was happening. Some barely moved as the women started removing their clothes. One of the soldiers – I could see his bones through his too-big uniform – kept folding and unfolding his arms. But others were starting to lose patience. A young soldier walked up to a girl and tore off her dress. "Hurry up!" he yelled.

Three Eyes started to do a little mocking dance, singing: "*Ma bele mingi, ma bele kitoko, ma bele, Mama.*" (There are lots of breasts, beautiful breasts, breasts, Mother.)

Our fear hung thick in the air. *Ya*Ziana looked around quickly and then turned her eyes to the ground. "Popina, Lola, do what they say and don't look up," she whispered urgently.

I started taking off the green dress that *Ya*Ziana had made for me and embroidered with tiny flowers. Scenes of the rebel men in the field just days before flashed into my mind. With a dull realisation, I knew it was about to happen again.

Next to me, hands shaking, Lola was removing her hijab, still covered in her mother's blood. The dead boy lay on the ground, flies already swarming around the pool of black blood that surrounded him. I wanted to run as fast and far as possible to the forest. Like that three-legged dog.

I want to die.

The thought came suddenly and clearly – a knowing that it would be better to be shot and killed in an instant like that boy than to be raped and tortured by these savage soldiers.

My body felt like lead.

Only five years old, but with no more hope, no more innocence.

The soldiers made us lie on our backs. I closed my eyes tight, willing my death wish to come true. The rebels ordered the captured men and boys – those from Zongo and Kumase and our other neighbouring villages – to rape us.

And then the soldiers also raped us.

*

Around me, desperate cries of women and girls. "We are your sisters! Don't do this! Please! Let our children go ..."

A woman is begging them not to touch her two daughters. Holding machetes to the terrified girls' throats, the soldiers make them watch their mother's rape. When the soldiers are finished, the sisters are forced to watch them kill her.

Next to me, *Ya*Ziana is wringing her hands, begging the two men in front of us not to touch Lola and me. She offers her body, they can do whatever they want with her if they don't touch us.

The men laugh. "We'll do whatever we want anyway."

Another loud cry – a young woman tries to fight back. A group of soldiers surround her, beat her, rape her anyway.

Then a man is on top of me, forcing himself inside, and it feels like every inch of me is tearing apart.

*Ya*Ziana is weeping. A soldier orders her to be quiet, reaches for his gun. "If you don't shut up, I will thrash you with this!"

The next man is on top of me. And then the next. And the next.

Then a boy I know from my village. He is just as terrified as me, paralysed. He is only five or six years old. He starts to cry, doesn't know how to do it.

So they shoot him.

At times, it feels like my mind is separate from my body. I don't feel anything, and it is eerily quiet. I look up and see a blue bird flying above.

Please take me with you, I want to cry. But then the moment is gone, and the pain and terror take over.

We are in hell.

"You better shut up or we'll kill all of you!" Three Eyes shouts against the cries of horror, fear and pain. He shoots into the air a few times – as if we need reminding.

And then his cellphone rings – Triiiii-iiiinng! Triiiiii-iiiing! Triiiii-innnnng!

"Good afternoon, sir …" he says, walking away.

I feel lightheaded. Then it is black.

*

I was raped by more men and boys that day than I could count.

I was so small, and it felt like my entire body had been broken apart, piece by piece. I hadn't had anything to eat or drink for days and I was exhausted. But the most painful part was being raped by my own people, men I had called uncle, boys I had played with in the village.

I don't know when we started to understand what was happening: that the men and boys would be forced to become soldiers for the rebels. But looking back, I now know this was their initiation into violence. As soon as they were in the camp, the captured boys and men were forced to rape their sisters, mothers, friends from the village. They wanted to make rebel soldiers out of the smallest ones, the younger the better so they could be trained to be violent. And those who could not, those whose conscience did not allow such depravity, were shot because they were of no use.

Our brothers, fathers and uncles couldn't protect us or fight for us. They could only do what they were told to do.

Three girls committed suicide that day. While being raped they reached for the soldiers' guns and shot themselves in the head. There was so much blood, so many lifeless bodies, eyes rolled back, skin changing colour as life seeped into the dust.

*

The sound of chanting: "Power! Power! Give them guns!"

The sun had almost set on our first day in the camp. The sky was a riot of purple and red. Cool air against my burning skin, billions of stars exploding in my eyes ... My senses were overwhelmed. It felt like a dream.

If only it was a dream.

Three Eyes raised his hand and the chanting stopped.

"I received a very important call this afternoon. The Democratic Republic of the Congo is going down. This will become our land as promised."

"Power! Power!" shouted the soldiers.

I wished for a machete to cut off my ears and drown out the voices. I wanted to cry, but there were no tears. I tried to swallow, but my mouth was like sandpaper.

Three Eyes raised his hand again to stop the noise.

"It's time for these boys to become real men! Prepare the fire!"

It was the second stage of the boys' initiation. They would have the letter "R" burnt onto their chests. And the horrifying chanting went on and on. "Power! Power! Give them guns! Give them the mark!"

Three Eyes lit a match and threw it down on the ground. It flared briefly before he stubbed it out with his black boot.

"Even the soil will fight for Rwanda," he declared. "War is coming. And this is not the first war. This country and its people have no sense of peace. The sooner we fight, the sooner we can bring the last man down."

A skinny boy, eight or nine years old, was the first to be branded using the piping-hot iron. The rebels pinned him to the ground, holding down his hands and legs. Three Eyes was the one to press the iron to his chest.

One by one, the captured men and boys were marked. We were all made to stand and watch. Two boys lost their lives in the process.

At the same time, the rebels cheered and drank, and some danced to tinny music that blurted from a stereo. But nothing could drown out the haunting cries of the boys and men.

In our culture, we had been taught that men don't feel emotions the way women do. But that day, boys and men shed tears of shame, their pride destroyed. In a strange way, their terror made me feel sorry for those who had raped me just hours before.

*

The branding seemed to go on for an eternity. My eyes grew heavy and my knees buckled. Kneeling, I leant against my sister's legs. After the effort of simply staying alive, I surrendered to exhaustion.

When I woke, it was dark, but everyone was still where they had been. The moon was bright and clear, a silvery white beacon in the dark-blue sky. I watched the moon for a long time, the only sound the chirping of the crickets.

And then a sweet voice, softly in my ears: *You're going to live, Popina.*

8

A day passed. Another one. At some point, but not soon, we were given plain *fufu* to eat. Time seemed to meld into a vacuum in which nothing changed.

We women and girls were confined to an empty tent without windows or mattresses. The rebels stood guard outside. There wasn't nearly enough space for everyone, these empty shells of women and children, now without husbands and fathers, all crammed together. We took turns to sleep on the floor, otherwise we sat or stood.

Our tent felt like a furnace. Sweat burst from my pores, pricking my skin. I tried to lick my lips, but my tongue was bone dry.

"Are you thirsty?" *Ya*Ziana asked, worried.

"No."

Every day, groups of rebels visited the camp, bringing with them cash, guns and diesel that they traded for the stolen girls and boys. We didn't know what happened to those who were taken. Our traumatised minds had us believe that their circumstances were better.

And sometimes the rebels demanded body parts. People would be dragged out of the tents, beaten up and then made to stand silently while the visiting rebels chose whose body they wanted. They were like gods, deciding who got to live and who would die.

Does anyone know we are here?

I waited my turn.

It became weeks.

*

This morning, like many other days, I stood in line. Lola and *Ya*Ziana were with me always. No matter what happened, I knew, whether I died or lost my limbs, we had to stay together. Even if our eyes didn't meet as we stood in wait, I knew they were always looking out for me.

Then a rebel was standing in front of me. He was holding a cigarette, a gun almost the same size as me hanging across his chest. Perhaps for the best, the terrifying fear I'd come to know made me go numb.

He grabbed my wrist and stared into my eyes. Then he shoved me aside.

"Her eyes are too small." Raising his voice: "I'm looking for eyes and a liver."

"This one isn't too bad." Three Eyes pointed to a woman to my left.

"That's what I need."

Two men grabbed the woman and forced her to the ground on her back. More men held down her head, arms and legs. Someone sat on top of her with a knife in one hand and a spoon in the other. He didn't waste any time before driving the knife into her eye sockets.

*

Dark clouds on the horizon but I do not long for rain; the angry sky reflects the evil around me.

*

The woman's torture seemed to go on forever.

Screaming, she writhed, clawing and kicking, tearing up grass and sand, gasping for breath. Yet, after every fighting effort she was pulled down again into the growing puddle of dark blood.

The tension grew. Somewhere a despairing voice shouted: "Why does she have to suffer like this? Why?"

After the rebels had removed her eyes, they put them in a cooler box. Then they cut out her liver. Having got what they wanted, they left her to bleed to death.

I couldn't take my eyes off the broken body, massacred by animals. I watched her take her last breath.

Did your life end now, Mama, or has it just started?

I started praying: *Oh, Mama Nisodin, where are you? Please cut me loose.*

Lola was being inspected. I held my breath.

And then instant chaos – a fight had broken out between the rebels and the captured men. A prisoner attacked the rebel who had gouged out the woman's eyes, seizing him by the throat as he tried to grab the rebel's gun. Just as the outraged prisoner threw the rebel to the ground, a shot rang out and the rebel let out a piercing cry. Within seconds Three Eyes had torn the rebel's shirt with his machete. Then he slashed the man's throat and cut into his chest. Before we could comprehend what was happening, Three Eyes was holding up the rebel's pulsating heart.

"This is what happens to weak men!" he roared.

I'd never seen a heart before. It was oddly shaped like some exotic poisonous fruit. Eerily, it kept pumping, as if wanting to escape.

The front of Three Eyes' shirt was drenched in blood as he summoned a cooler box. In his hand, the heart kept moving.

In the chaos, Lola had run to me and grabbed my hand. Her eyes these days were dull like muddy pools. My head started spinning. A rebel was staring at me – one moment he was the right way up, then he was upside down. My eyes couldn't focus. He raised his gun and aimed at me. I started shivering.

"You two!" He pointed his gun at Lola and me. "Get back in line!"

I felt Lola's hand tighten around mine, but as we got back in line a rebel pushed *Ya*Ziana to her knees, his gun at her chest.

"Please! Please! No!" she begged.

A wave of panic came over me. The rebel lowered his gun, then raised it again. Worse than the fear of death was the feeling of not knowing what was about to happen. He yanked *Ya*Ziana back to her feet and shoved her towards our tent.

Her cries soon told us what was going on.

*

The dark clouds had formed an ominous canopy above our heads. A single drop of cool rain rolled down my nose, and soon it was pouring. The rebels started dispersing – there would be many more opportunities to lord over us.

We ran for cover.

In the tent, *Ya*Ziana was on her knees, naked. "Please …" she begged the rebel in a low, scratchy voice, as if this single word had taken all her energy. The rebel zipped up his pants and left.

Lola covered *Ya*Ziana with her *liputa* and we sat quietly next to her, listening to the rain. *Ya*Ziana stared blankly upwards, slowly rocking back and forth.

"A lot of people died today," someone said.

"The soul never dies," *Ya*Ziana replied softly.

I was in shock. What was happening around us day after day was incomprehensible. So many people mutilated, killed, taken who knows where. The camp smelt of dead people, of rotten bodies – you could almost taste the stench. So many people had been ripped from our lives: Mama Nzembo and the friends and families we had shared our days with, and people from villages we barely knew.

For the next few hours of that day, between muted coughs and murmurs, someone would let out a wail – a sound of sorrow but also of rage. Lone voices rose up from bodies covered in different hues of blood; fresh blood was the brightest red. I wanted to cry but I couldn't. I needed every ounce of energy simply to survive the next minute, the next hour.

And I was determined to survive. *I will survive if my sister is with me*, I told myself. I would survive by attaching myself to her like a shadow.

Lola held *Ya*Ziana's hand but *Ya*Ziana barely seemed to notice as she swayed back and forth.

*

By the afternoon, the rain was still coming down in buckets when four armed boys barged into the tent. Mafuta was now leading them, looking like some tiny new-age soldier in a torn black shirt, too-big green pants with a black belt and large dark glasses. He pushed his way to the middle of the tent and stood in front of Lola.

Mafuta was only a boy, but he was one of the rebels now. Having been initiated, he had his own crew – a bunch of seven- and eight-year-olds. We saw that the rebels liked to put children in charge, and we learnt especially to fear the small ones – because they were the ones without conscience. The young rebel boys were running their own fiefdoms now, and the adults only interfered when things devolved into chaos.

Mafuta had always been a bully, and he'd always had a grudge. Now he also had power and guns.

He grabbed Lola's hair, forcing her to face him.

The other boys grabbed two women and threw them, screaming, out of the tent, and before I knew it Mafuta was dragging out Lola, and me as well. The rain was falling so hard that the sound blurred into a whirring noise. The downpour had created red puddles around the many dead bodies still lying outside.

"I told you your time would come!" Mafuta yelled at us.

He ordered some of the other boys to strip us down but we didn't want them to touch us so we removed our clothes ourselves. They made us lie on the ground, face down, while they bound our wrists and feet with rope. Mafuta instructed one of the boys to bring him a plastic pipe.

And then he started lashing my cold, wet body. He commanded the boys to hit the other women too.

"Harder!" he yelled.

My wet skin amplified the impact of the long, thin pipe. My body quivered with every strike.

"I'm sorry, Mafuta! Please! Please stop, Mafuta!" I pleaded.

He must have struck me twenty times before he switched to Lola. She received even more lashings.

It was as if he was possessed. "I'll smack you until you wish you were in hell!" He demanded we apologise louder, saying he couldn't hear us.

The other boys threw down their pipes. "We can't beat these girls any more, Mafuta."

But he threatened them, ordering them to go on. When they refused, Mafuta turned to the women and struck them even harder.

By now I'd stopped screaming. My head rested listlessly on the ground; I might have drowned in the pool of rainwater. Blood ran down my sides from the cuts on my back.

"Enough!" Three Eyes shouted and Mafuta immediately dropped his pipe. "Take these girls back to their tent," the older soldier demanded.

They pulled us back to the tent – I had no strength to walk. My body was numb from the pain. As I lifted my head, I caught a glimpse of a man I knew as Makambo's father sitting in the rain, hovering over his son, his body small with grief. The rain was falling around him in a relentless torrent, but he remained unmoved by its chill. "He won't breathe! My boy won't breathe!"

The rain was a steady cascade of sorrow. It may have washed the blood from the soil, but it couldn't wash away our despair.

Back in the tent, *Ya*Ziana held my hands but she barely moved. She kept her eyes downcast, her lips pressed closed. We noticed another body lying motionless in a corner – no one knew how or when she had died.

We sat waiting for the next onslaught. There was nothing else we could do.

The pain of those wounds would last for many weeks.

*

In the silence, I am aware of my empty stomach. We have not eaten for days, and there is no sign that food is coming. Starvation is setting in.

I close my eyes and daydream. I can smell *Ya*Ziana's cooking, can almost taste her hearty soups and stews, and the memory brings some comfort. I decide to believe that, if I hold on just a little bit longer, someone will rescue us. We will return to our village. We will feast on *Ya*Ziana's cooking.

An ant is walking across my foot. As it makes its way, I impulsively reach out and put it in my mouth. I can feel its legs tickling my tongue as it scurries around. I start to chew, then swallow, feeling the morsel slide down my throat.

It is surprisingly satisfying.

I grab another ant and examine it before giving it to Lola. She accepts reluctantly but puts it in her mouth. It isn't long before the tent erupts with women and children crawling on the floor, digging through the dirt, looking for ants.

*

Gunshots pierced the air outside.

Everyone in the tent held their breaths, the smell of sweat and dirt.

More gunshots, then excited shouts from the returning rebels. They had captured more boys and girls and were celebrating their victory. Their joy in stark contrast to the violence that would follow. These were the worst days. Blood always flowed on these days, and there were a lot of days like this.

In our tent we looked at one another in disbelief.

More captives. More terror.

My clothes were wet. *Ya*Ziana reached out and pulled Lola and me closer. Shivering, we huddled together listening to those children's cries.

A voice in my ear: *Everything will be alright.*

I closed my eyes, saw myself floating in comforting darkness.

There I felt calm. As young as I was, I knew that I found my true self in this darkness. That no matter what was happening, I could come back to this place to find solace.

Everything will be alright.

9

The rain continued for several weeks, turning the forest around us into a muddy marsh.

It was a miserable time.

Once in a while the rebels would realise that their prisoners were withering away and would share their *fufu* with us – the only highlight of our time in the camp. The rest of the time we filled our stomachs with water and whatever walking or crawling insect we could find on the ground around us. The few spoonfuls of *fufu* tasted like pure heaven compared to the bitter insects.

The one thing we could rely on was the constant fear.

Will I be next? The next one butchered for my organs? The next one raped or used as entertainment when the rebels are bored? The next one traded to go work in the mines?

Stories from the mines were frightening. Many of the children from my village, some as young as seven or eight, had been sent there. We heard that they worked long hours in extremely hazardous conditions, forced to carry heavy loads, do intense digging and handle machinery. They were exposed to toxic dust and chemicals. Tunnels would collapse, killing people instantly or leaving them crushed, dying a slow, painful death in the dark.

Lola had become thin and weak. Her cheeks had lost their rosy glow, and she looked frail, as if she could simply dissolve, become a heap of bones. And me, when I reached up to touch my head, I would find myself staring at a handful of hair.

The wounds from the lashings on Lola's and my backs were taking a long time to heal. We had tried our best to clean them, but they only seemed to be getting worse. *Ya*Ziana worried that the wounds were infected. Lola's skin was worse than mine – it was red and inflamed, as if her skin was rising in anger.

There was just one reprieve: every now and then the rebels allowed us outside the tent. We would huddle together in the rain, soaked but treasuring the feeling of water on our faces. Maybe we believed that, like the rain, our suffering would eventually end.

*

Today the rebels were celebrating.

From the tent I watched as they laughed and cheered, dancing the *kwassa-kwassa*. A few boy soldiers sat in a circle, smoking cigarettes and taking swigs from bottles they were passing around, liquor dripping from their faces. They seemed blind to the corpses lying around, immune to the stench that hung like thick smoke in the air.

One of the new captives approached to ask if they could dig holes to bury the dead. The rebels discussed this for a few moments but decided the dead should be left as is. They waved the man away and continued drinking and smoking.

But the man was desperate – and brave.

"Please! Let us respect the dead and bury them so they can rest in peace. I beg of you! Allow us to give these men, women and children a last resting place."

We held our breaths as the rebels considered this. Finally they agreed that the captives could bury their dead, and the man quickly called for shovels. Soon the captive men were gently lowering bodies into the ground.

People I knew. Children I had played with. I was overcome with sadness.

*

Later that afternoon, we were allowed outside. It was overcast but dry and the air was cool and refreshing. I watched the lush, vibrant trees around us swaying gently in the light breeze. It would have been tranquil if we were sitting outside our hut back in the village.

A movement above Lola's head. A flock of birds gliding across the sky.

Where are they going? Can I climb on their backs and fly with them, like magic? As they reached the horizon, they became silhouettes.

But then I was filled with an urge to hunt the birds, grab a bird out of the sky, sink my teeth into it, crunch its bones, sweet meat filling my mouth.

*Ya*Ziana appeared with a bottle of rainwater for me. Drinking it was bliss.

*

Five women were dashing towards the forest, towards escape. They ran with desperate, almost supernatural speed, but the rebels were quick to follow and corner them.

These women weren't going to give up. They fought the rebels with every ounce of their energy. They shouted, they screamed. One woman was tall and beautiful, and she fought like a hunter, her energy fierce. When her efforts seemed fruitless, she didn't back down and the other women seemed to take courage from her.

But it wasn't enough. The rebels overpowered them.

"Kill them!" Three Eyes shouted. "But leave the tall one."

He walked over to where the brave woman was lying on the ground, breathing heavily. He walked slowly around her, then grabbed her by the neck, lifting her off the ground. He held her face close to his, staring intently into her eyes.

"What kind of woman challenges a man?"

The once-strong woman was hung from a tree and left to die.

Her strength had given me the courage not to give up. I found myself crying for that woman as if I had known her.

*

We were outside when Lola collapsed. Losing no time, *Ya*Ziana rushed over to her, checked her breathing and her pulse. She rubbed Lola's back and chest to try to stimulate her breathing.

I knelt down next to *Ya*Ziana, desperate to help.

"She's so hot," *Ya*Ziana said, but I couldn't tell the difference between hot and cold.

*Ya*Ziana lifted off Lola's top and looked at her back. Her hand flew to her mouth when she saw Lola's infected wounds.

*Ya*Ziana started pleading with the rebels to allow her to go into the forest to find healing herbs. "Please! I know exactly where to find them! It won't take long. You can come with me and watch me. I can get extra to treat the other people." Her voice was eerily high, but the rebels simply ignored her. What was another life, especially that of a small, fragile girl?

*Ya*Ziana turned her attention away from them.

"Bring water! Now! We need water!" she shouted.

Bondeko, one of Mafuta's village friends, rushed towards us with a bottle of water. I hardly recognised him – over the months in the camp he had grown taller, his skin was darker and his facial features had become more pronounced.

How long have we been here? I wondered.

Bondeko knelt next to me and poured water onto Lola's face. Then he tried to get some into her mouth.

"Slowly, slowly," he said gently. His voice, I noticed, was deep as a man's.

Lola started to regain consciousness. Soon she was thirstily gulping the water.

"Be strong, alright?" Bondeko said softly to Lola. He lifted her into his arms and slowly carried her to the tent. Once he had carefully laid her down, he looked at me. "Watch her while Ziana and I go look for herbs in the forest."

I lay down next to Lola. It was clear she was in a lot of pain. I took her hand in mine and closed my eyes. My mind started wandering, and I thought back to how we had played in the forest, going home too late in the evening with pockets filled with sour mangoes.

"You need to fight, Lola," I whispered. "Fight so we can go back to our favourite mango tree."

Tears were rolling down Lola's cheeks. "Mama, Mama," she said softly.

Was my mother still alive? I wondered. Had she been captured too? Had the whole world been captured?

With silent tears we lay next to each other, presence the only thing we had to share. She knew I loved her. In the quiet tent, I prayed for a miracle.

"Is your sister back yet?"

The female voice startled me. A woman was standing over me, holding a baby. She was rocking the baby side to side.

I jumped up. "No, but she'll be back soon."

The woman kept rocking the baby as if in a trance.

Hours later *Ya*Ziana and Bondeko returned with the herbs and more water. *Ya*Ziana rubbed the herbs between her hands and then knelt down, tenderly turning Lola onto her stomach. She started rubbing the herbs onto Lola's back. Then she gave me a few leaves and told me to chew and swallow them.

"Give me some as well, I beg you." It was the woman with the baby. "I need to breastfeed my baby."

Bondeko leant over to see, but then stepped back. "Why is your baby blue?"

"Devil, leave my son alone." The woman's voice was trembling. "He's just hungry."

*Ya*Ziana took the baby and cradled him in her arms. She gently moved him up and down, but the baby was still. No sound, no movement. She held him closer, softly talking to his tiny face as if willing him to wake up. But the baby remained motionless.

Tears welled in her eyes. "Your baby is gone," she said in a low voice.

"He is not – he just needs food. If you can give me some herbs to eat, I'll be able to make milk."

No matter what anyone said, the desperate woman kept repeating that her baby was alive. Her eyes pleaded with us to understand. She held him close and whispered into his ears, begging him to wake up. She kept asking for herbs, her grip on the small body getting tighter and tighter.

"We cannot waste these herbs," *Ya*Ziana said calmly. "It took a long time to find them, and I need to look after my little sister."

I ate the herbs she gave me. They tasted bitter, almost pungent, but I got used to it the more that I ate. I chewed as *Ya*Ziana rubbed more of the herbs into the wounds on my back. Her hands were warm. I felt the pain starting to subside.

When she was finished, *Ya*Ziana looked at me.

"It's going to be okay," she said, taking my hands in hers. "I'm here for you. Everything will work out."

Without warning, the woman holding the dead baby lunged and grabbed *Ya*Ziana's arms. Distraught, she sobbed, desperate for the herbs so that she could feed her baby. Bondeko tried to calm the woman down, but she collapsed on the floor, her body shaking as she held her son's body to her chest.

I could see then that she knew she had lost her baby. *Ya*Ziana wrapped her arms around the woman and offered to take the baby so that she could rest. But the woman didn't want to let go. Lola, Bondeko and I sat in stunned silence, watching the woman mourn. I sat down next to her and put my arms around her neck, and she clung to me as she wept, her pain radiating.

We stayed there until her tears had stopped, and eventually Bondeko stepped forward and took the baby from her arms. I looked at the tiny boy, so still and cold.

Bondeko suggested we bury the baby. His voice was kind.

But a disturbing thought entered my mind: I was hungry.

Horrified, I put my hands to my ears, shook my head, and to my relief *Ya*Ziana asked me to take care of Lola while they buried the baby. The grieving mother went with them, leaving Lola and me alone in the tent. I didn't want to tell Lola that I was scared, so I just held her hand and kept watching the tent opening, willing no rebels to come inside.

Lola lay trapped in her pain and eventually the others returned.

"We're going to see who else we can help," said *YaZ*iana, picking up the remaining herbs.

Soon after they had left, Lola broke her silence.

"I love you, Popina. Remember how we used to race from the river to the village? We were happy." She smiled faintly.

I felt my heart swell. "But you used to cheat."

"I had to, otherwise you would win."

We both knew things would never be the same, but in that moment we felt like ourselves again. I made a funny face, and Lola giggled so I got up and danced until I had run out of breath. I fell down next to her, exhausted but happier than I'd been in a long time.

"Popina, where do dead people go?"

I thought for a moment.

"Well, *YaZ*iana says we go to a much better place. If you have a good heart while you are alive, Mama Nisodin will transform you into a beautiful tree that gives life and shelter to birds and animals in the forest. If you die as a warrior, she will grant you life in another form and you will walk the earth like a god."

We fell into silence. When I next looked at Lola, she was staring at the roof, eyes wide. After a while, she blinked.

I knew Lola wasn't okay.

"Mama and Papa, where are you?" She was looking up, talking in a low voice. "*Oyo ezali mokolo mpo na yo. Nandimi Nzambe, oteyaki ngai nandimaNazali komituna soki nakomona yo kala mingi te …*" (This is you, God, I agree. You called me and I am here and I can't wait for the day I see you …)

I couldn't make out her exact words. She would pause, take a breath, and then continue talking. When she looked back at me, it was as if she was looking through me. There was a strange light in her eyes.

"What are you thinking about, Lola?" I asked, but she didn't answer.

When will I die? I wondered. *Will it be painful? What will happen to me? What will I transform into?*

I wondered if I would take memories of people with me, or if memories also die. I started feeling angry – angry that death was inevitable. And I felt hopeless.

Is death the only way out of this misery?

But death scared me.

A soft voice in my ear: *It's not yet your time.*

It was the voice I had heard before. Gentle, reassuring. And my fear started to fade.

I replied back to the voice: "Mother Nisodin, if you can hear me, give me the courage to break free. I pray for freedom."

The voice was quiet, but I knew my prayer would be answered because I felt a sudden burst of energy and strength.

I was ready. I was ready to be free.

10

A week had passed without any rain. Although we were grateful to be dry and warm, the rain was our only source of water for drinking and washing. We would collect rainwater in large buckets and drink it straight from there. The women had decided among themselves that those who were having their cycle were allowed one cup of water to wash themselves – before we had that rule, one or two people would use up all the water to wash themselves. When the rain stayed away, the stench in the tents became unbearable.

We were asleep in the tent when shouts from Three Eyes and his men jolted us awake. They came in with whips and started beating us, yelling at us to get up and get ready – they had big business today.

Lola, who was lying next to me, was too weak to stand. Her breathing was shallow and her skin sickly pale. *Ya*Ziana and I had to carry her outside to where the rebels told us to line up. She was trembling, mumbling under her breath.

The rebels were counting us when Lola collapsed again. I tried to help her up, but the rebels yelled at me to leave her. I stepped back and watched as they dragged her away – I didn't know where.

A rebel I didn't know was talking to Three Eyes. He was tall and skinny, dressed in a green army jacket and pants with black boots. He was holding an AK-47, which he stroked with his one hand as if it were a baby. He had an air of authority about him, even though his eyes were hidden behind a pair of dark glasses.

"I need ten of your strongest kids for the mines," the man said. "We lost some in a collapsed tunnel."

Three Eyes gestured for some of us to form a new line. "Take your pick. In exchange for guns, of course."

The man started surveying us one by one, as the tension around me thickened.

Stopping in his tracks, the man swerved towards Three Eyes. "I need boys," he said angrily. "What am I supposed to do with these?"

"There are some boys. And you know both girls and boys can be good mine workers," Three Eyes replied. "In fact, girls are often better."

I closed my eyes, a new wave of fear washing over me. I had to stay with Lola, make sure she got stronger. The dread was overwhelming.

I was staring at my feet when I realised the cold barrel of a gun had been pressed against my forehead. I slowly looked up. The man's eyes were small and sharp, like a rodent's.

"What's your name?" he asked abruptly.

"Popina," I said in a small voice.

He asked me to spell it. I replied that I didn't know how to spell. He laughed and asked how old I was. I told him I didn't know that either, although I might have been six by then.

He lowered the gun and commanded us to do push-ups. I had no idea what he was talking about, so I just stood there, confused. Some girls around me dropped to the ground and started doing the exercise, so I tried to copy them.

Doing push-ups when you're starving and exhausted is not easy – I could not get my body off the ground. The girl next to me was also struggling. She started with her knees and feet on the ground like one would stand on all fours. She lowered her chest towards the ground and then slowly pressed herself back up, using both her arms and legs. Between each push-up, she took a break, her breath coming in short, laboured bursts.

The two boys on my other side were stronger, but I could see they were pretending to be weak to avoid being chosen. They took long breaks, groaning as if they were in great pain, and their movements were slow and strenuous. Their efforts were futile. The rebels commanded them to line up for transport to the mines.

Out of nowhere, I felt a sharp pain in my back. I spun around – the tall rebel had hit me with the butt of his AK-47. "You wouldn't even make it there. The mines are not for the weak – get back to the other line!"

I nodded in agreement, my heart still pounding in my chest. Scrambling to my feet, I hurried back to *Ya*Ziana's line.

Three Eyes approached the tall rebel. "Have you found what you need, John?" He sounded nervous.

John. It was the first time I had ever heard that name and I wondered what it meant.

I lined up next to my sister feeling utterly alone even though all around me I could sense those who had suffered, fought and died. I tried to shift my focus to the wind in the trees, the smell of earth. I closed my eyes and prayed for strength.

Because what if tomorrow *did* come?

When I opened my eyes, I knew I would survive this darkness. I would keep going, one foot in front of the other. No matter how hopeless it seemed.

I took my sister's hand and squeezed it. She squeezed mine back.

After the first selections had been made, the chosen boys and girls were separated. A little boy about my age was sobbing uncontrollably, his small body shaking with each breath. The black shorts he wore hung like an oversized skirt over his skinny legs; his eyes were wide in his ashen face. His mother was pleading with the rebels to take her instead and the boy was clinging to his mother, begging to stay with her. But the rebels were unmoved. On the mines, the smallest ones were the best for getting into holes.

One of the girls chosen that day was Benedict, my friend from the village whose rock rabbit Lola and I had played with. Benedict had always loved exploring the forest looking for animals. Now her face spoke of utter defeat. She and the boys who'd pretended to be weak walked off like zombies, as if in a trance. That was the last time I ever saw her.

As the children were taken away, a collective wail erupted from the remaining captives and echoed through the forest. I held tightly to *Ya*Ziana, tears streaming down my face.

A tall woman I didn't know came up to me. She was wearing a brown dress, her feet were bare, and she seemed gentle but fierce at the same time. She put her hand on my shoulder and leant down to me.

"No matter what happens," she said, "never forget your courage."

"Bondeko, take them back to their tents!" Three Eyes shouted.

Around me, the other captives were standing like statues, faces shiny with tears.

Bondeko appeared, accompanied by more rebels, and instructed us to walk back to our tent. We passed a few dead bodies. The smell was putrid – they had been lying there for days. But my disgust didn't obscure my gnawing hunger.

I forced myself to look away, told myself to hold on a little longer.

*

As I walked into the tent, I saw Lola on the ground – the rebels must have brought her back. But she wasn't moving, and people were starting to crowd around her.

Bondeko ordered them to get out until just he, *Ya*Ziana and I remained. Then it dawned on me.

I started screaming: "*Yaya*! *Yaya*! Lola isn't waking up!"

I shook her body in desperation. Her infected back was a braid of sores in angry colours. The infection had crept its way up her neck, encircled her ears. Sections of her dress clung wetly to her wounds and a bad aroma emanated from her skin.

The child in me held a tiny glimmer of hope – maybe she was just sleeping. I shook her again, shouted her name as if my voice could reach her. "Lola! Lola! Lola! Lola!"

Coldness seeped into my bones as I gave in to sorrow like a rock inside me. Between her own tears, *Ya*Ziana was telling me it would be alright, but we both knew that nothing would ever be the same again.

*

*Ya*Ziana left me and I don't know how long I sat there with Lola, rubbing her hands. Was I hoping that my love would give her a reason to fight her way back to the world?

When darkness fell, I was forced to let her go. Lola, my best friend, my soul companion. *Ya*Ziana knelt down and slowly pulled me away from the body of my friend.

*

It was Mafuta who came to remove Lola's body. Seeing him, my anger boiled. He was the reason Lola was dead – his beatings had caused the wounds on her back. I rushed towards him and pushed him with all my might. Using only one arm, he simply pushed me back.

"Girls like you need to be taught a lesson, Popina," he said. "You're next if you don't behave."

He and Bondeko removed Lola's hijab, picked her up and left the tent. I felt as though a part of me had been ripped away.

Could I have saved her? Why wasn't I strong enough to stand up against these boys? As they left the tent, I felt a vacuum of despair. My throat was raw, and the burning in my eyes made me realise that my tears hadn't stopped.

*Ya*Ziana held me. "Look at me, Popina. We will get out of here. I've been having dreams, visions of a woman and a crowd. I don't know what it means, but that will become clear. It will be our salvation."

*

Another day. Shouts from outside and two rebels barge in. They seize *Ya*Ziana and me by our hair and wrench us apart and out of the tent. They heave us across the camp, our bodies bruised and battered by stones as they drag us over the ground and into the forest.

The rebels pull apart my little legs. Turning my head, I lock eyes with my sister.

They are angry with *Ya*Ziana – watching me will be her punishment.

Briefly they get caught up in a fight among themselves about who will go first. They take turns at me, playing their twisted power game.

I lie there. I feel detached. In the midst of it, I force myself to look into their eyes.

Then I think of Lola. I envy her.

11

I only realise now how close to starvation I was. There was a time when I would lie awake at night in the dark tent and could hear the otherworldly sounds of my stomach above snores from the other captives, as if my body was trying to consume itself from the inside.

The hunger was constant, no matter what other terrors we endured. Whether I was being beaten by the rebels, made to help bury bodies or being inspected for other unknown horrors, the void was always there. How much longer would I be able to survive?

Another day with only water. Fainting from weakness.

Somehow, I was determined to stay alive.

*

Dusk was falling, the sky's deep blues and greys both beautiful and ominous. Shadows from the giant trees grew longer and longer, making me uneasy. The air was heavy with humidity and the earthy scents of the forest, and it clung to my skin, weighing me down.

Looking at the ground, I spotted some ants. Without a thought, I grabbed the tiny black insects and put them in my mouth. It was as if they dissolved before they even reached my stomach, and then the hunger was back.

Someone had lit a fire, and the captives were sitting nearby. Even the young ones' faces were weary, their cheeks hollow, their eyes lifeless – shells of humans on the brink of survival. No one talked.

There was one man – his hair was wild, creating a black halo around his head, his face rugged. There was dried blood all over his arms, but I'd long stopped wondering where all the blood came from. We wore each other's blood like a uniform.

Nearby, two teenage soldiers were struggling to move three lifeless bodies one by one away from the fire. When the bodies were lined up, the young rebels looked at one another, their eyes serious. Perhaps the bodies had been friends in their previous life.

As if materialising out of thin air, a few older rebels were suddenly commanding us captives to undress – as they often did. We started removing our clothes and I noticed the wild-haired man get up. But instead of undressing, he approached the dead bodies with eerie calmness. I was frightened for his sake, but everyone was too scared to say anything.

The man reached into his pocket, fumbled for a small knife with a smooth ebony-wood handle and intricate patterns on the blade. He must have stolen the knife – captives could not carry such things.

Everyone was looking at him. Even the rebels seemed paralysed.

The man knelt down at the body of a little girl in a bloodied orange-print dress. I recognised her – I found out later that she and her older brother had tried to escape. Some of the new captives had been forced at gunpoint to beat the siblings to death with sticks, and then smear the victims' blood on their arms as a reminder. The wild man must have been one of them.

Now he carefully lifted the girl's dress.

Bending closely, he gently touched the skin of her thigh.

*

The smell of cooking meat from the fire. The horror.

The rebels are glued to the spot, their faces contorted in disbelief, unwilling or unable to interfere. Witnessing something worse than their own brutality has rendered them dumb.

The man removes the meat from the fire and takes a bite.

Watching the man, people scream – "You animal!"

One of the rebels shouts in Lingala, and they start moving towards the man.

I am hypnotised. Desperate. I start feeling a strange connection to the man. His actions don't repulse me. Instead, I am salivating.

I rush past them all and reach the man first.

*

My senses started returning. When I opened my eyes, the other captives were surrounding the man.

"*Mtoaji wa maisha!*" Giver of life.

Extending their hands.

And so, in one evening, cannibalism became part of life at the camp.

12

One day, as we were sitting eating around the fire, Three Eyes came rushing towards the rebels, talking excitedly. We couldn't make out what he was saying, but it must have been good news because shouts of joy erupted.

We understood at the time that the rebels already had power over a significant portion of the northern region of the DRC, and their power was increasing. Their target was now Businga, a town in the Nord-Ubangi province.

Three Eyes started dancing around the fire as if nothing could stop him. He had a radio with him and he started relaying to the others what he was hearing: the rebel forces had successfully seized the city of Zongo on the northern border with the Central African Republic. They had driven out a large number of opposing rebels from Businga. The defeated rebel group was now moving west to Gemena.

The next update was also shocking: around three hundred Congolese-government troops had flown into Bangui, the capital of the Central African Republic, and were poised to launch a counter-attack on Zongo from across the Oubangui River.

Planting his feet firmly on the ground, Three Eyes lifted a bulging fist into the air and shouted: "War! War! War!"

The rebels responded with their own chant: "*Toko boma bango. Congo eza yabiso!*" (We're going to kill them all. Congo is ours!)

These impassioned men made me sick. On top of their violence and strange mystical beliefs, they now seemed to believe that eating their victims gave them special powers. The rebels had started wearing human body parts as trophies.

*

We were sitting around the fire. We hadn't eaten in days. The rebels were cooking the last of the meat, but it was only for them; and they would probably make us watch them eat it.

Through the crackling flames, I spotted a three-legged dog emerge from the forest, drawn by the scent of the cooking meat. The thought struck me, *He's alive!* It must have been the same dog I'd seen the day I arrived, so long ago now.

At first, the dog's movements were tentative. In the flickering firelight I saw his spotted red coat, a mosaic of scars. A survivor.

I watched him slip between us.

There was something vulnerable about him. Perhaps sensing his longing for companionship, *Ya*Ziana called to him and he came over, tail wagging, and started licking her face. *Ya*Ziana stroked his face, spoke softly into his ears.

"We should call him Red Dog," I said.

She smiled and was about to say something when a rebel seized the dog by its neck and stabbed it.

We could only watch in silent horror as the rebels killed and dissected the dog, starting with removing its intestines. Soon the air was heavy with the smell of raw meat as the rebels prepared and then portioned it out to be cooked on the fire.

No one said a word until one of the captives spoke.

"At least it's not one of us."

How could we be forced into this – the eating of people and dogs? If the only alternative was dying, did we even have a choice?

We accepted our portions with hunger and reluctance. The meat wasn't like anything I'd ever tasted, and a murmured debate started about whether it tasted more like chicken or game. Eventually, though, we fell silent.

*

The days melded into one another, blurring into a continuous cycle of survival. Keeping track of time seemed a luxury for the free world. Each day unfolded in a monotonous succession of efforts to sustain and protect ourselves.

The tally of lives became a haze. Butchering bodies – human and animal – was now an accepted necessity. Some of us maintained an unspoken code: before we ate, we gave thanks for the sacrifice. But there were times when I found myself unable to abide the taste.

And then it got even worse.

Initially, only the bodies of those who were already dead were eaten. But it soon became clear that a body that had lain in the sun for a few days was not fit for consumption. That's when the rebels started killing captives for food, capturing them while they were sleeping. We would sit down to our weekly meal terrified that we would be next.

I said many prayers.

The fear started taking over my mind, casting a dark shadow over my days. By this time, we all knew that survival often came at the cost of our own humanity. Was it only a matter of time before I found myself on the wrong side of this struggle?

One night we were abruptly torn from sleep by a man's harrowing cries – "No, please! Not me! Somebody, please help me!" A collective fear and empathy stirred among us, but no one dared move. We could only listen and pray.

Waking from uneasy sleep the next morning, I remembered the terrified voice of the man in the night. I rushed to the opening of the tent.

In the pale glow of daybreak, the man's lifeless form was suspended over a crackling fire. His clothes and shoes lay discarded on the ground, flies hovering.

In the afternoon, portions were distributed.

The taste was now familiar. Numb acceptance.

It's strange how someone can become stronger and weaker at the same time.

*

"I had another dream," *YaZiana* said. "Of that woman standing in front of a crowd. The people were cheering. I tried to move closer to get a better view, but I couldn't get through the crowd."

YaZiana's dream hung in the air.

"What does it mean, *yaya*?" I asked.

"I don't know yet."

I couldn't remember the last dream I'd had. I had stopped dreaming. Yet we believed dreams carried a unique power, especially in the darkest times. Sitting with my sister, I longed for such sanctuary.

Years later, I would dream about the people I ate during that time. Especially the first one, the girl with the orange dress. These were always nightmares.

13

Life and death. Black and white. One or the other.

As time passed and the first horrific months turned into years, I found that the line between life and death can be obscure, and it can be difficult to know who is alive and who is dead. Many of those who had passed remained with us in spirit, while those who were alive carried the essence of death, as if everything but their bodies had already given up.

In the camp, the living and the dead shared much the same existence. In such close proximity, illness and disease spread like wildfire and we were always battling some infection, as if death was constantly trying to get its grip on us. When someone died in the night, no one had the strength to haul them away, so a motionless body would remain among us like an omen.

I was now ten years old.

*

Night had fallen and we were lying outside, close to a fire the rebels had lit. *Ya*Ziana was next to me, holding my hand. The never-ending terror had taken its toll, and we were permanently exhausted, profoundly empty.

Looking up at the tapestry of stars above, *Ya*Ziana broke the silence.

"They are maps, you know. They can lead us to another world," she whispered. "Every star has a story, and these stories make up the whole universe, way beyond our small world of horrors."

"How many worlds are there, *yaya*?"

"More than you could ever imagine. When you are older, I'll teach you how to read the stars." *Ya*Ziana smiled in the dark. "Before I came to our village, my school taught us not only about the forest but also about the mysteries of the night sky."

I could almost hear the whispers of the ancient tree, the rustling of forest leaves back home …

The moment was shattered by the rebels' raucous laughter. Singing along to distorted, ear-splitting music from their boombox, their revelry drove them to stomp around the fire.

My sister fell silent. We were used to this – our lives were completely in the rebels' hands and everything worked around them. But even between captives connection was met with hesitation, averted eyes, recoiling bodies. People had built up their own protective walls, and some had become informants. No one was to be trusted.

Suddenly, there was scuffling and panic, a cold scene playing out around the flickering flames. The drunken rebels were making the women and girls dance with them, and they were even more forceful when they were met with resistance and tears. We were trapped in an eternal cycle of humiliation. Tonight, like many others, the rebels forced alcohol down our throats until we gagged.

I wanted to creep away unseen but Mafuta pulled me up from the ground, grasping me tightly around my waist. He was older now – about fifteen – and up close his breath smelt of rotting plantain.

The rebels' chants grew louder as they demanded more beer. I realised in panic that I'd lost sight of *Ya*Ziana and I also couldn't think straight. I found myself shoved into the circle of music. Mafuta was smirking at me, not loosening his grip.

"Dance, Popina!"

I forced myself to move, but I felt more hatred with every step, every sway. As the song reached its height, the rebels raised their voices.

I caught sight of two girls standing together, surrounded by men. It wasn't long before the rebels had dragged them into the forest, their pleas evaporating against the night's cacophony. The foliage beyond the camp swallowed them in an instant.

And then I saw *Ya*Ziana, her hair and clothes ruffled as she tried to break free from the rebels dragging her towards a tent. As they disappeared inside, my heart ached for my sister.

It took a moment before I realised that Mafuta had stopped dancing and was reaching for my face with his coarse hands, pulling me towards the dark forest.

A heavy stone settled in the pit of my stomach as the music, the laughter and cries were replaced with the rustling and haunting of the forest at night.

Deeper and deeper we went.

He stopped next to an enormous tree. Its twisted branches reached out as if to touch the moon.

"Why did you bring me here?" I asked, trying to calm my racing thoughts.

"Shut up, little girl!" He stepped closer. He leant forward to kiss me but I bit his lip and he slapped me with such might that I fell to the ground.

Then he took out his knife and bent down, pointing it straight at me.

"If you don't do what I say, I will kill you." He kicked me. "I always said your time would come!"

In prying open my legs, slapping me as I tried to fight back and undoing his pants, he put his knife on the ground. In a split second, I grabbed it and stabbed him below the belly button with all my strength.

Mafuta froze in shock. I stabbed him again. Again. And again.

He fell on top of me. I shoved him off and climbed on top of him, pushing him down with my knees as I kept stabbing.

I only paused when he stopped moving.

*

A whisper through the stillness, tender words like a gentle breeze: *Even death cannot separate us.*

"Lola …" I whisper back into the night.

Out of nowhere, a figure. To my astonishment it is my sister, and she signals me to stay quiet. Then I hear it: voices and hasty muffled footsteps. The rebels are looking for her.

I hold my breath as they come closer. *YaZiana* crouches down and takes my hand, her eyes darting as she calculates our options, her whole being attuned to our surroundings. Only once the footsteps fade do I dare breathe.

The forest is silent before *Ya*Ziana slowly gets up.

Then she sees Mafuta.

*Ya*Ziana stares at him, then looks at me. A silent acknowledgement.

In the dim moonlight, we work together to drag him under a bush. He is wearing the copper bracelet worn by all the boys in our village. His father would have given him that – they said it was good for the bones, to keep them straight.

I feel a strange emptiness.

Searching his pockets, *Ya*Ziana finds a gun. For a moment she stares at the weapon in her shaking hands, then she tucks it into the folds of her *liputa*, fastening it securely around her waist.

*

I don't know why we didn't run. We didn't think we could leave; we were scared of being free. Perhaps we had forgotten how to live.

"We need to get back quickly," *Ya*Ziana whispered. "But no one must see us."

No one but the moon. Using its subtle light, my sister led the way. We were on high alert; every whisper an echo to our ears. We used the tree-shadows to stay hidden.

Near the camp we crouched behind some bushes until *Ya*Ziana motioned that we should approach. The captives and soldiers were still gathered around the fire. We moved slowly, step by step, hearts pounding, and silently entered our tent.

When we came close to the spot where we usually slept, our gazes simultaneously fell on Lola's hijab. It had lain there for many years – our only possession. A comforting and haunting reminder. *Ya*Ziana picked up the hijab and held it out to me.

A sense of shock washed over me.

"We have to hide your dress," *Ya*Ziana whispered urgently. "It's got blood all over it."

Realising I had no choice, I carefully pulled off my too-small green dress. It took all my strength to pull Lola's hijab over my head – every inch of fabric felt like her. But there was no time for more grief.

We scanned the tent for somewhere to hide my dress, and our eyes fell on the pile of tattered and blood-stained clothes that had been worn by those who had died. We carefully buried my dress, though the pain of losing it nearly made me weep.

As quietly as we had entered the tent, we made our way back to the campfire, praying that our absence hadn't been noticed. As we emerged from the shadows, the fire's glow seemed almost inviting, despite the tension in the air. Cautiously, we tried to blend in with the others.

The rebels' young faces appeared gaunt in the light of the flames, and they were speaking in hushed tones. We kept our distance but tried to listen to what they were saying. *Ya*Ziana's grip on my hand tightened.

Then, without warning, a group came rushing from the forest. "Mafuta's missing!"

Despite the warm air, their words sent a chill down my spine.

*Ya*Ziana's eyes searched the crowd, vigilant. Had anyone seen us? As the rebels' cries subsided and they started earnestly discussing the situation, three adult figures joined them, seemingly out of nowhere. One was Three Eyes, his gaze sharp and calculating as he took in the scene. Uncharacteristically, he was wearing mismatched, worn-out clothes, but his authority was undeniable as he stepped into the circle of younger rebels.

When he raised his hand, everyone fell silent. The only sounds were the crackling fire and the night animals. Then he shouted a command that cut straight through my soul. "Search the forest! We are not sleeping until we find him!"

The rebels immediately scattered, disappearing into the shadows.

An eerie silence fell on those of us who were left. The forest seemed to hold its breath, the silence broken occasionally by distant shouts.

Three Eyes remained at the fire, his scarred eye fixed on the path into the forest. The dancing flames cast strange shadows on his face. Hand in hand, *Ya*Ziana and I watched and waited. Then, Three Eyes and his two commandos turned towards us captives, scrutinising our faces as if they intended to extract all our secrets simply by looking at us.

We stood frozen to the spot. Three Eyes stepped forward, the other two rebels behind like a shadow. He shifted his gaze to *Ya*Ziana, taking in every detail. Then he stepped closer, his face right in front of hers. I shuddered. For a moment, the moon seemed to dim. A gasp escaped *Ya*Ziana's lips as Three Eyes leant in and licked her cheek, leaving a trail of lingering disgust. When he spoke, his voice was chillingly calm.

"You taste guilty."

14

"I know who killed Mafuta!"

It was a few days later. There had been whispers around the camp about Mafuta's disappearance, and now I recognised the voice – it came from one of the most senior rebels, a big man with a wild beard. When I looked up, my blood turned to ice.

He was dragging *Ya*Ziana towards where Three Eyes and his rebels were sitting drinking and smoking.

"This whore is responsible. She's the one!" He shoved her into the circle of rebels and she fell to the ground.

Three Eyes put out his cigarette and slowly got up.

He looked at the bearded rebel. "Why do you think she is guilty?"

The man pulled something from his jacket. He was holding Mafuta's gun.

"She was hiding this in her clothes."

I felt faint.

Three Eyes took the gun from the bearded rebel and slowly turned it in his hands. Then, in one swift movement, he pushed the gun into *Ya*Ziana's face.

"No!" My voice erupted before I could think and I ran towards Three Eyes. The sound of my scream echoed in my own head as I collided with another soldier.

Movement, sound, colour – as pandemonium erupted, the gun was fired.

What was happening? Another nightmare? I couldn't make sense of anything.

*Ya*Ziana grabbed my arm, pulled me onto her back and started running. We didn't have a plan. We just knew this was it.

*

*Ya*Ziana stops to catch her breath. She puts me down and grabs my shoulders, still gasping for air.

"We've got to run, Popina!"

The air right behind us explodes with gunfire. *Ya*Ziana pulls me along as the noise echoes all around. I am stumbling.

"Don't look back!" *Ya*Ziana screams. "We're going to die if you don't run!"

Tightly gripping my hand, my sister propels me into a dense patch of forest. Our hearts pound in sync with the footsteps following us.

More gunshots, each round more frightening. I keep falling; the rebels keep getting closer.

"*Yaya!*"

*Ya*Ziana pulls me onto her hip like she is carrying a baby, tells me to hold on around her neck. Bullets fly around us. Cradling me with her left arm, my sister pulls out Mafuta's gun and starts firing back. I tighten my grip as her bare feet thud through leaves on the forest floor.

A few minutes or an hour later, the darkness beneath the tree canopy seems to swallow us.

In the new silence, I hear the familiar voice: *Don't look back.*

Without stopping, *Ya*Ziana shifts me onto her back, holding me there with both hands. Against my face the cool night air is comforting. I close my eyes, surrender ...

Until *Ya*Ziana trips over a rock and we both tumble to the ground. Leaves scatter like tiny insects.

Trying to catch our breaths, we can still hear the rebels looking for us. *Ya*Ziana lifts me onto her back again but she now needs one arm to navigate the uneven terrain.

The rebel sounds are growing louder. Are we slowing down? Going in circles? The leaves crunching beneath her feet also sound like gunfire, but *Ya*Ziana increases her pace. I cling to my sister, feeling the thud of her heart against my own chest.

Then, a sanctuary: a colossal tree with intertwining roots that form a little cave. We slide into this refuge.

Inside the tree-cave it is cool and dark. Minutes tick by.

How long have we been running? How far? We huddle close together, feeling each other's pounding heartbeats. Distant sporadic gunshots remind us there will be no mercy.

"Try not to even breathe," my sister whispers.

How far are they? In which direction are they going? We don't dare move.

The voices start to fade but we remain frozen.

One wrong move and it is over.

*

A long time had passed since we'd heard the voices. The tension began to untwist.

Instead of the rebels' haunting shouts, we became aware of the gentle symphony of the night forest, creatures that had probably been there all along.

"I'm tired, *yaya*."

I could feel that she wanted to keep running, wanted to increase the distance between ourselves and the dreaded camp. But she didn't want to push me too hard. And we had no idea where we were or where we should go.

It was the first time in five long years that we were free.

"I know you're tired, *popi*. We'll sleep here tonight."

For years we had slept every night on the hard ground, but now my sister started gathering fallen leaves to create a soft sleeping place for me. I slipped into my sister's arms and she stroked my head.

"Early tomorrow morning, before the sun has risen, we'll start our journey to South Africa. They say that it's safe there."

"Where is South Africa, *yaya*?"

"South – I don't know where exactly. But it is calling me."

Our new beginning floated into the night.

2005–2006

DRC, Zambia, Zimbabwe, Mozambique

15

Emerging from our dark shelter just before dawn, it took a moment for our eyes to adjust. The air was fresh. I saw that we were surrounded by colossal trees, an army of motionless giants.

As the sun peeked over the horizon, *Ya*Ziana pointed. "Do you see that?" she asked. "That's east. If we want to go to South Africa, we've got to go south-east."

As if accepting its duty as compass, the sun suddenly broke through a strip of low-lying clouds, painting the sky in soft pink and gold.

There was no time for a breath.

We had to run.

*

Hours later my stomach is cramping from hunger and my bare feet hurt. I ask *Ya*Ziana if we can rest and look for something to eat.

"No – we will rest at midday," she says, adamant. "Better when it's hot."

We run on. An endless race.

To distract me, between breaths, my sister tells me about the stars, explaining how they guide us. Having learnt navigation at school, she gestures with her hand, pointing out the cardinal directions: east, west, south, north.

"You must remember ... that women are considered ... the creators of this world ... That's why ... we are taught its secrets ... And that's why ... Mother Nisodin will bless us ... on this journey."

That idea feels important – that women and nature are connected, and that this knowledge has been passed down through generations.

I feel part of something.

*

After the first day, we stopped running. But as we would discover over the months, even walking wasn't easy.

It was a long way to South Africa and we had nothing – no shoes, no warm clothes for the cold valley nights. I was still wearing Lola's light hijab, and my sister wore an old shirt and her *liputa*. Her *liputa* was what kept me warm at night – she would wrap me in it to sleep.

And we had no food so we would eat grass and raw grasshoppers. Sometimes *Ya*Ziana would find lizards to eat.

We'd seen no signs of water for days after our escape. Now, for what seemed like the hundredth time, we stopped to pull thorns from our aching feet.

"Are we almost at South Africa?" I asked, sure we had covered a great distance.

"Not yet," *Ya*Ziana replied patiently. "But we will get there if we keep walking. Then you can go to school."

The forest floor was dense with fallen foliage, making it hard to spot rugged stones and living dangers like snakes. I had quickly learnt to follow *Ya*Ziana, to step only where she had stepped, as we had in the forest near our village.

Another day: "*Yaya*, I need water! I'm thirsty!"

*Ya*Ziana spun around, grabbing my shoulders.

"Look around you, Popina! Just take a look." She was impatient for the first time since our escape. "The trees also need water; the animals and the insects need water; *I* need water. So, who are you to complain?"

I didn't ask again. I tried to lose myself in the rhythm of our footsteps, concentrate on putting one foot in front of the other.

It would be better if the rebels had caught and killed us, I thought to myself. With such intense hunger and thirst, we were not much further from death than we'd been in the camp.

But we pressed on.

*

*Ya*Ziana stopped in her tracks.

"A river! I can hear a river!"

She started running in the direction of the sound, and I followed. It wasn't long before we got our first glimpse. Water – a most beautiful sight.

It was a huge river – very wide, with many tributaries and wide sandy banks. But our elation was quickly dampened: in the shallow river's edge, lurking just below the water's surface, were the ominous shapes of crocodiles.

If we were careful we could perhaps sneak to the bank for a quick drink, but it would surely be impossible to cross. Yet the rebels, like us, were north of this river, and our journey lay to the south.

"*Yaya*, how will we cross the river?"

For a while we stood staring at the deep green water and the crocodiles. Then *Ya*Ziana removed the gun from her *liputa* and handed it to me.

"I'm going to test how deep the river is. Then I'll come back. Stay here and don't move."

*Ya*Ziana started cautiously walking towards the bank.

I stared down at the gun, the textured grip dirty from all the different hands that had used it. The weight of it, of what it had done ... Overwhelmed, I dropped it and let out a scream.

Around me, as if in reaction, leaves rustled, the river rippled, the forest birds went silent. In a flash, *Ya*Ziana was next to me, covering my mouth.

The crocodiles' unnerving eyes were on us.

My sister looked at me, her eyes a fiery warning. She picked up the gun, placed it back in her *liputa* and steered me further down the river. When she was satisfied that we had found a relatively safe spot, she urged me to kneel down and drink some river water while she kept a lookout. Then it was her turn.

The bank was covered in tall grass and when *Ya*Ziana had finished drinking I noticed that it was teeming with insects. I didn't think twice – in a frenzy I started picking them off the grass and shoving them into my mouth. I didn't even know what I was eating. *Ya*Ziana joined me, and for a while we felt satisfied, almost happy. But as much as we wanted to, we couldn't stay here. *YaЗ*iana said that our next step was to cross the wide river.

"Most of the crocodiles are over there." *YaЗ*iana gestured behind us.

"But I can't swim, *yaya*," I pleaded, but she was already making her way towards the water.

"If we die today, or tomorrow, or the day after, then so be it. At least we tried to reclaim our own lives. Do you understand, Popina?"

I looked down. "Yes."

"Good, that's my girl. Now get on my back and hold my neck as tight as you can. Don't be scared; just hold on."

Slowly we entered the river. But *YaЗ*iana had underestimated the current, which was soon pushing us in all directions. When the riverbed suddenly dropped, *YaЗ*iana had to start paddling.

*

Battling to keep her head above water, my sister is struggling. My arms can't hold on.

I lose my grip; I am surrounded by water.

I can't see *YaЗ*iana.

I'm terrified of crocodiles. I scream.

I'm sinking, deep, deep. I open my eyes to the rushing darkness. Everything is strangely calm.

That voice again: *Not today.*

I see a bright-green light. I reach to touch it.

The softness of *YaЗ*iana's hand pulling me out of the water.

*

I have no idea how long it took to get to the other side of the river and all its tributaries and side streams. When my sister laid me on the far riverbank I wasn't breathing properly. My chest burnt and I vomited water, feeling as if my lungs were being torn apart.

Gradually my breathing returned to normal, and once *Ya*Ziana was satisfied she carried me away from the water, putting me down in the shade of a big tree. The heat was scorching – there was no way we could continue walking.

*Ya*Ziana suggested we rest here for a couple of days, until I had regained my strength, so we tried to make ourselves comfortable. We built a fire with kindling and bamboo. That night and the next we slept under the stars, a feast for the mosquitoes that tormented us.

It wasn't long before my body started to tremble with chills, only to be hot with fever the next moment. *Ya*Ziana quickly recognised the signs of malaria. She knew we needed medicine – holy basil has always been used against such symptoms.

"I need to find some *tulsi*." She gently covered me with her *liputa*. "It's very strong medicine."

She placed a handful of dead grasshoppers beside me, covering them with leaves.

"Don't eat them all at once."

Then she placed the gun into my trembling hand. I would never get used to this instrument of death in my hand.

"Popina, if anything or anyone comes near you, you defend yourself. If you don't shoot, you'll die." She closed my fingers around the gun. "If I'm not back in two days' time, you must carry on by yourself, okay?"

And she was gone.

*

Here, beneath an ancient tree somewhere near a river in a vast forest in the DRC, I wait for my sister. I lie as still as I can, hoping that will ease my pain.

I watch the sun move across the sky, see birds flying against clouds.

But my pain and fever are getting worse.

"Lola, is that you?" I ask the air. Suddenly, I sit up. Was that Lola's scream?

Something catches my eye. A snake sliding towards me. A python.

Panic surges. I use every bit of control to stay as still as possible. My heart pounds.

Can the python sense my fear? It's close to my feet now.

I hold my breath.

It changes direction and slithers away.

*

On the first day, I lay as still as I could until it started getting dark. Then I knew I would have to make a fire. After eating a few grasshoppers, I got up to find kindling.

With the flames and warmth I felt safer, but the feeling didn't last. As it grew darker, rain began to pelt down. The fire I had built with such effort flickered and died, and the forest closed around me like a suffocating blanket. I felt tears well.

"*Ya*Ziana, please come back," I whispered.

"*Yaya*, please come back!" I shouted, but the heavy rains swallowed up my voice.

I hugged my knees to my chest, trembling with cold and fear.

"Please, *yaya*, please come."

*

On the second day, I woke staring into the bright-blue eyes of a small, golden-brown monkey making the most comical sounds.

I was about to greet him when I saw that he'd snatched the gun while I was asleep. He seemed to understand his crime because he started running away with it.

"Bring it back!" I shouted as loud as I could, following him weakly.

The monkey seemed to think it was a game. He kept moving back in my direction, almost within reach, before darting away again and into a tree. I scolded him but then I saw that it was a fruit tree!

I started picking fruits from the branches I could most easily reach and then I sat down, losing myself in the invigorating, juicy sweetness. Eating was bliss. When I eventually made my way back to our camp, I was surprised to see that the monkey had followed – still holding the gun.

"You can stay as long as you don't use it," I told him.

But I was starting to feel nauseous and dizzy, and before I knew it, I was vomiting. Then, between heaves, I became aware of a loud thumping sound overhead.

Something I didn't recognise was flying in the air – a giant bird with no feathers or ... a strange-looking aeroplane. The strange plane had one long arm at the top that was moving in fast circles. And then the all-too-familiar sound of gunshots.

*Ya*Ziana! Where was she?

The commotion had also startled the monkey and it had darted away, taking the gun with it.

The thing kept circling overhead and the gunshots grew nearer. Heart pounding, I scanned for a hiding spot. There was a dense clump of trees – I ran for cover, hands over my ears.

Should I just lie still and hope I'm invisible, or should I risk it all and run for my life?

Has Mama Nisodin abandoned me?

Even after the noise had faded, I didn't dare move. In the absence of gunfire, the silence was deafening. I remained frozen, waiting for some sign that it was safe to emerge from my hiding place.

Minutes stretched into hours. Another night passed.

*

On the third day, I woke up feeling stiff and confused. It took a few minutes to remember what had happened.

*Ya*Ziana should have been back by now. Had something happened to her? Or had she given up on me? Should I continue on my own? Or should I hold on to hope?

I didn't know what to do. Then I realised that she wouldn't know where to find me in my hiding spot. As I tried to get my body to listen to my brain, I became aware of a voice calling.

"Popina! Where are you?" *Ya*Ziana's voice was frantic.

I scrambled to my feet and started running towards the voice. And there she was, through the shadows, her face streaked with tears, her voice hoarse from calling my name.

I rushed into her arms.

"I'm back," was all she could manage. Then: "I'm so sorry, my *popi*."

It took a while before she was ready to tell me the story.

"While I was looking for herbs, I noticed a tree full of birds. Do you know what that means, *popi*?"

"It means it's going to rain."

"No, it means there are eggs! So I climbed up to look for a nest, and I reached one that had four small eggs inside. I was so hungry I ate two of the eggs right there in the tree – everything, Popina, even the shells! But while I was up there I noticed a thin trail of smoke in the sky, and when I followed it I saw a cluster of huts. A village, Popina!"

*Ya*Ziana's words were now tumbling in a rush.

"I wanted to get back here fast to tell you, but I lost my grip and I fell out of the tree. It was so painful I didn't think I could stand! But I could hear baboons all around me and they were coming closer. So I forced myself to get up and run."

I took a closer look at her leg. It was bruised, clearly injured. "*Yaya*, how are you going to walk to South Africa with that leg?"

"It will heal fast. Nothing's broken." She gave a reassuring smile but I wasn't convinced. "Anyway, I was stumbling along when I heard a helicopter. I hid under a tree as it passed overhead. And then there were gunshots all around me, and I could hear people shouting. I just prayed to Nisodin that I wouldn't be caught. It went quiet but I wasn't sure if it was truly safe, so I stayed in my hiding spot until today."

"I saw it too! I didn't know it was a heli … a helichopper."

"Helicopter."

"And I also found a place to hide."

"Clever girl," my sister said proudly. "Now it's time to get you better."

While we slowly walked back to our campsite, I told *Ya*Ziana how the monkey had stolen the gun. She just shrugged. "We'll be okay without it."

Back at the camp, *Ya*Ziana looked for rocks to grind the seeds of the *tulsi* plant she'd found. It was then that she came across the gun – the monkey must have dropped it.

"At least we still can defend ourselves," she said. Shaping a leaf into a makeshift spoon, she scooped up some of the herb paste. "Here, eat – it will make you stronger."

It was strange, wild-tasting.

"We can't stay here, Popina," *Ya*Ziana said earnestly. "We have to find that village. It might take us a day or two to reach it. Maybe we'll get some food and clothes there."

The herbs were making me drowsy. She picked me up and positioned me on her back like a very small child, securing the gun again in her clothes.

Exhausted and hurt, she started walking in the direction of the village.

16

I don't know how long we walked. Every now and then I tried a few steps on my own, but I was still very weak.

Dusk was fast approaching and the sky had turned a greyish blue when we finally saw signs of village life. As it got darker, *Ya*Ziana had to step more carefully to make sure we didn't both fall.

Then, out of nowhere, a woman's voice: "Who are you?"

*Ya*Ziana froze and looked around. But there was no one in sight.

"Who are *you?*" she asked back.

"Why are you walking this way with a little girl on your back?" asked the voice. When *Ya*Ziana didn't answer, a woman emerged from between the shadows. "Is the child injured?"

She was tall and graceful, her hair braided in an intricate pattern.

*Ya*Ziana briefly explained our situation, leaving out the part about the rebels.

"Aha, so the little girl is sick, poor thing." The woman spoke with an accent and I struggled to follow her. But *Ya*Ziana seemed to have no problem – she'd learnt to speak Swahili in the camp and knew many local languages.

"My name is Celine. Let me help you carry her," the woman offered, stretching out her hands.

*Ya*Ziana put me in her arms. "Thank you, Mama Celine."

I knew I didn't look well. I was small and malnourished, my cheeks were sunken, my eyes had dark circles around them. My hip bones were visible through my dress and I was drenched in sweat.

It felt as if my throat was lined with wood and grass; speaking was painful.

We set off towards the village, and I slowly became aware of the sounds and smells of everyday life. Soon we were inside the woman's hut, which was homely and warm. After so many nights in the forest, having walls and a roof overhead felt safe.

"How long has she been sick?" asked Mama Celine.

"It's been about a week now, and it seems to be getting worse."

"Come, sit for a moment. I have the right herbs to help your little sister. She will be fine."

Mama Celine started preparing the herbs.

"So, where are you heading?"

"We're going to South Africa, for school."

The woman looked up. "For school? I'm sure you can find a school in one of these villages. Why put your lives in danger for school?"

*Ya*Ziana straightened her back. "It's not *just* for school. Our village was destroyed, and we've been held captive in a rebel camp for five years. We escaped. Your village is not safe; they will come here too – rape the women, kill the weak and abduct the little girls and boys. So we are going to South Africa, to freedom."

Mama Celine didn't seem surprised by my sister's warning. "How do you plan to get to South Africa?"

"We will walk."

Mama Celine handed my sister a wet rag, indicating that she should dab my forehead.

"You should stay here tonight. You are very welcome."

Her face was open and honest, and her large eyes shone in the candle-light. She went outside to place the small pot of mixed herbs on the fire.

"You're the first people to come to our village in a long time," she said when she returned. "We heard that the rebels had taken over up north near the borders. And there's still a war between the Dinka and the Nuer. Two months ago a few boys from South Sudan passed through here, accompanied by an elderly man. They were also heading to South Africa. They said that the Murahaleen raiders who terrorised villages in Sudan were from Darfur."

She paused to light another candle.

"Mama Africa is dying. We are dying every day. It's the curse of the African people – death, poverty and suffering. The oppressors live in abundance while their victims endure severe hardship."

Mama Celine got up and walked back out to the fire area. She started dishing up bowls of stew and brought them to us. There were tiny pieces of meat floating on the top. Memories of our diet in the camp surfaced.

"You need the nourishment," *Ya*Ziana reminded, seeing my hesitation.

I obediently chewed and swallowed, and soon I felt the strength seeping back into my body.

Mama Celine handed me a bottle of water, and we ate and drank in silence until *Ya*Ziana spoke again.

"What's the name of your village?" she asked Mama Celine.

"Boso-Lengo," Mama Celine replied. "You should be able to reach Kinshasa on foot in a few weeks. The Sudanese boys were also heading for Kinshasa. They were hoping to find a truck heading to South Africa."

Part of me wished we could stay here in peaceful Boso-Lengo.

After we had finished our meal, Mama Celine went to fetch the herb mixture from the fire. She poured some into a small container and instructed me to drink it.

"You might feel dizzy at first, but tomorrow you will wake up strong."

After I had drunk it she covered me with a blanket, and it wasn't long before I felt my eyes getting heavy. It was quiet, I was warm and my stomach was full – perhaps I had, in fact, died and gone to heaven. I tried to force myself to stay awake to enjoy this dream. But eventually I succumbed.

*

I woke up with a bright beam of sunlight streaming onto my face. I'd dreamt about Lola, but then I remembered that I was sleeping in a strange place.

I reached for *Ya*Ziana, but she wasn't there.

"*Habari za asubuhi*," said a strange voice.

My head jerked up. I was staring into the face of a boy. He was taller and bigger than me, and he was wearing an oversized shirt and shorts kept in place with a black belt.

Smiling, he said something else. Had I heard right? Had he just called me "sunshine"? *Ya*Ziana's admirers had called her that in the village. I touched my almost bald head – malnutrition had taken most of my hair.

The boy must have seen my confusion because he repeated in a singsong voice: "Hello, sunshine!"

That's also what the rebels sometimes said before they ...

"Touch me and I will kill you!" I yelled.

Slowly, he raised one hand and knelt down, placing a bowl of rice on the ground.

"I won't hurt you. Mama Celine just sent me to bring your food."

I grabbed the bowl and started eating. The boy turned slowly, walked over to a water container and poured some water into a tin cup. He held it out to me, and I took it and drank. He tried to move closer, but I moved back.

"Good morning, Popina," Mama Celine said as she and *Ya*Ziana returned to the hut.

For the first time in years, *Ya*Ziana had changed her clothes – she was now wearing black pants and a red top with "Coca-Cola" written on the front.

"*Yaya*," I exclaimed in amazement, "you have shoes!"

"Here's a pair for you too." She handed me a pair of sandals – too big, but I was so happy.

When Mama Celine gave me a dress and a big blue jersey, I was almost dizzy with excitement. Then she pointed to the boy.

"Popina, this is my son. Michael, did you give her some food and water to drink?"

"Yes, Mama, but this girl is crazy – she wanted to attack me!"

Mama Celine just shrugged and asked Michael to bring in some bathing water from outside.

When *Ya*Ziana and I were alone, my sister helped me to wash. The hot water on my skin was soothing. Then she helped me put on my new clothes. It was bittersweet because the new clothes meant I had to take off Lola's hijab.

"It doesn't mean you're losing her," *Ya*Ziana assured me. "You don't have to wear Lola's dress to carry her in your heart."

"Michael's going to show you around, Popina," Mama Celine said, returning to the hut. I could hear young children playing outside and I looked at *Ya*Ziana.

"Yes, go," she said.

Outside, it almost felt as if I was back in our village. There were children playing, some racing on makeshift carts. There were chickens roaming, pecking at the ground, and in the fields around us the villagers were tending their gardens and crops.

"Are you alright?" Michael asked as I stood and stared around me.

I nodded, curious but also apprehensive.

We walked a bit further and were soon surrounded by children who must have been about the same age as me, although I felt much older. They looked at me with bright eyes.

"*Bonjour*! I'm Sarah," a girl chirped, extending her hand.

"And this is David, and that's Emily."

They introduced themselves one by one, eager to make me feel welcome. Before I knew it, we were chatting away like old friends.

"Would you like to come and help us pick mangoes?" Sarah asked.

I looked at Michael, who hesitated for a moment. "Okay, but we're not allowed to go far," he cautioned, and I suddenly felt grateful for Michael.

And for picking mangoes.

*

We made our way beyond the village to where the wild mangoes grew. Once there, caught up in the moment, I grabbed mango after mango from the trees. When we'd collected our bounty, we started to eat. Succulent and sweet, the juice dribbled down my chin.

"Delicious!" said Emily.

"Hey, slowly, Popina," Sarah urged. "You're going to choke or get a stomach-ache."

Her words brought me back to reality and I grinned at her.

"So, where are you from?" she asked.

The question lingered in the air – I didn't know how to answer or where to even start. Then Michael said it was time to leave and we all started walking back to the village. I kept thinking about Sarah's question: Where *did* I come from?

I would think about that later, I decided. For now I would just enjoy walking back to the village with friends after picking mangoes.

Something so ordinary. So completely extraordinary.

*

Back in the village, everything felt peaceful and the sky was just starting to fade to a soft golden pink. I realised that we must have been out all day.

Inside Mama Celine's hut, *Ya*Ziana was packing a plastic bag of food. Another bag stuffed with clothes stood nearby.

"We're leaving first thing in the morning," she said to my unasked question.

"South Africa," I said, a statement more than a question.

*Ya*Ziana nodded.

"What is South Africa?" The question came from Michael.

Mama Celine handed me another cup with the herb mixture to drink.

"You've never heard of the people of South Africa, my son?" she asked. "And do *you* know the story, Popina?"

And so Mama Celine told us the story of South Africa, the times of oppression and struggle, of resilience and triumph. She told us about Nelson Mandela, a name I'd never heard before.

"He led the fight against apartheid," she said. "He was put in prison for twenty-seven years and then became president of the country." She told us about his belief in the power of unity and his call for all Africans to build freedom together as one people. As she spoke, I felt I could see this Mandela's vision as clearly as if it were my own.

"Nelson Mandela is you. He is Michael. He is Ziana. He is me," Mama Celine ended.

"How is that possible?" Michael was frowning, but I felt inspired – her words had spoken to my heart.

"Now, Popina, come help me dish up."

Mama Celine had prepared a traditional dish called *pondu*, a savoury stew made with cassava leaves and spices, simmered to perfection. Alongside it we had fish from the nearby river, fresh and flaky. To complete the meal there was steaming-hot *fufu*. The flavours of home wrapped around me like a warm, familiar embrace.

"The last time I ate like this was in our village," I told Mama Celine. "My sister is a very good cook."

*

Suddenly, I see a vision. I'm in a tree picking mangoes when Lola appears. I am frightened at first, but then I look at her smiling face, and I feel safe.

I have often imagined Lola being with me, protecting me, but this time is different. She is moving, talking, nodding her head as if to tell me she really is here, that she can hear me.

I become aware of *Ya*Ziana gently shaking my shoulders.

"Hey, where are you?" she says, and I carry on eating my *pondu* stew.

But Lola appears again, this time looking for her Quran, asking if I have seen it – "Popina, where's my book?"

"I can't talk to you now, Lola. You must go away."

"I can't leave until I find my book. I never finished studying it!" She starts to cry. I get up and walk towards her – I will help her find her book. When I get closer, I see that it really *is* Lola, just the way she looked in the village, seven years old, with her beautifully radiant eyes.

When I try to explain to her that she's just a vision, she laughs. So I start laughing too, and then we talk about our village, laughing until tears stream down our faces.

We leave the hut and go walking outside, just like we did when we were younger. The air is cool and crisp, and the stars shimmer above us like tiny diamonds. We stroll down the familiar streets of our village, and it feels as if each step is a bridge between the past and the present, that the frayed threads of time are being spun together.

A distant voice is calling Lola's name. It's her mother, summoning her home to read the Quran.

Lola's face lights up. "My book – my mother has it! It's not lost!" Then her excitement turns to sadness. "It's time for me to leave."

I nod. I understand how important this is to her.

"I'll walk you home," I offer, not ready to say goodbye.

When we reach her hut, Lola turns to me.

"Thank you for today." With a final wave, she disappears.

*

"*Popina*!" *Ya*Ziana's voice. "Hey, wake up. You need to finish eating so we can sleep. We have to leave early tomorrow."

I rubbed my eyes and looked at the two packed plastic bags on which our survival depended. Fruit, nuts, seeds, water, rice. Some warm clothes. Was it enough? But it was more, far more, than we had started with.

*Ya*Ziana finished packing while Michael unfolded the sleeping mat. He and his mother had given us their hut. They would sleep at their relatives.

Despite our weariness, *Ya*Ziana and I both knew we had to keep moving. As we settled down, my mind was racing.

"Goodnight, Lola," I whispered.

17

The rain poured steadily, turning the footpaths into mud that clung stubbornly to my sandals, which became heavier and heavier with every step. There was no use trying to wear them – I was battling to keep up with *Ya*Ziana as it was. Walking without shoes might have become normal for us, but being barefoot for so long caused huge blisters. In the mud our feet swelled up and worms now lived in our soaked and water-cracked skin.

We had changed our plans and decided to head towards the city of Kisangani in the centre of the country, where the Lualaba and Congo rivers meet, because it was closer than Kinshasa. But it was not close enough. We'd been walking for days on end.

And then it became weeks.

Weeks and weeks through this dense and never-ending forest, past huge trees full of monkeys – always monkeys, monkeys everywhere – marshes full of ferns and impenetrable bush. At every new hill I would tell *Ya*Ziana that I couldn't any more.

"You see that far mountain over there?" she would say. "When we get to that mountain, you can rest." But for every mountain we reached she had a story about why we needed to keep going.

*

The several groups of armed men we encountered as we neared the city of Kisangani should have warned us, but when we finally reached the city, it was chaos. It felt like the rebel camp, but many times bigger, which was a shock after so long in nature, with just each other. There were armed soldiers everywhere, tanks patrolling the streets and locals who all seemed in a frantic hurry. We quickly learnt that many people had the same goal as us: to secure transport to Kinshasa.

And there definitely weren't enough vehicles for everyone. Those with money at least had some negotiating power. But our pockets were empty.

We turned into a side street to avoid being trampled by another convoy of tanks. Ahead of us was a bus, and next to it stood an old man yelling at the top of his lungs.

"Kongolo! Who needs to go to Kongolo?"

The bus looked old and battered. The faded paint was peeling off, and some of the windows were cracked.

"Kongolo! Kongolo! Who is looking for transport to Kongolo?" the man shouted.

I was about to ask *Ya*Ziana where Kongolo was when she turned to me, grabbing my shoulders urgently.

"We can go to Kongolo! It's in the right direction at least."

*Ya*Ziana rushed towards the man, pulling me along. Then she slowed down and took a deep breath before walking up to him.

"Papa, I am here with a child," she said softly, indicating to me. "We need to get to Kongolo, but we don't have any money." There was a slight quiver in her voice.

The man looked at her and narrowed his gaze. Then he looked at me. Without taking his eyes off me, he asked her how old I was.

*Ya*Ziana hesitated before replying: "She's ten."

The old man's smile widened, revealing a set of crooked, yellowed teeth.

"She can be the payment," he said matter-of-factly.

We both stared at the man in disbelief. *Ya*Ziana tightened her grip on my hand.

"She's just a child!" she pleaded.

"Do you want to go to Kongolo or not?"

*Ya*Ziana exhaled and stepped closer to him, delicately brushing her fingers against his shoulder. "Of course, papa, of course we want to go. And I understand your need for payment ... But what about me, hey? Am I not pretty? I have more curves than this little one." She moved her other hand across her body.

The man looked at her but didn't reply.

"I will make it worthwhile for you," *Ya*Ziana persevered. "I know how to make a man feel good. What would this little girl know? She hasn't yet learnt the secrets of how a woman can please a man."

"No, I want her," the man demanded.

I looked at *Ya*Ziana, saw her face twitch.

"I'm telling you, papa – you'll regret that. I'll do whatever you want me to do. In fact, I'm feeling particularly adventurous today ..."

"It's a simple question: do you want to go to Kongolo or not?" the man repeated.

*Ya*Ziana turned to me, tears in her eyes.

"Listen, *popi*, I need you to be brave one more time," she whispered. "It's our only chance of getting out of here, of getting to South Africa. We have nothing else. Just think of the future."

For a moment I was furious at my sister for selling me to a stranger. But I realised we were in a desperate position. And I was already numb to what would once have been unthinkable.

Without saying a word, I nodded.

*

We followed the man to a small room close to where the bus was parked. The room was mostly empty, except for a bed and a large plastic bag in the corner overflowing with clothes.

*Ya*Ziana gestured for me to take a seat on the bed.

"It will be okay," she whispered. "I'm staying right here."

The old man wasted no time. He'd already removed his worn-out sneakers and was now clumsily unfastening his belt.

"*Ya*Ziana, I can't ..." I sobbed.

"I know you can. Think of yourself in a classroom in South Africa," she said. "Think of building freedom. Think of anything but here and now." I knew she was trying to be brave. "Just one last time, *popi*."

The man's pants dropped to the floor.

I crawled into a corner but he was surprisingly strong and he easily overpowered me. When I stopped screaming, the other sounds became amplified: the rustle of fabric, the man's heavy breathing, the creaking of the bed, *Ya*Ziana's sobs.

When he was done, as the ultimate act of degradation, he urinated on me, warm liquid on my skin and a suffocating odour. Getting up, he threw a dirty shirt at me and commanded me to wipe myself, as if the horrors done to my body could be erased by a piece of cloth. *Ya*Ziana rushed to my side and helped me to clean myself.

"In South Africa, this will be something of the past," she whispered, but tears were still streaming down her face and I knew she hated herself for what she had allowed to happen.

There was nothing left for me to say, but in spite of the deadness inside me I heard a familiar voice: *Not today, not tomorrow.*

Having dressed himself, the man tossed my sister some money, instructing her to buy something to eat.

"The bus leaves for Kongolo in twenty minutes. If you're late, I'm not waiting."

My sister grabbed three big jackets from the pile of old clothes and put them in a plastic bag to take with us. She found an old empty bottle, which we filled with water.

Taking the money, we bought some dried tilapia and pap. Returning to the bus, we saw that people were starting to cram in but we managed to get two seats in the middle. It was the first time I had ever been on a bus, and in a strange way I felt a twinge of exhilaration, of expectancy.

While we waited to leave, I looked out of the window at the whirlwind of activity in the street. Families were moving hurriedly, barefoot children carrying loads that were too heavy for their small frames, some begging for food. There was a protest going on nearby, people raising defiant voices above the chaos. I spotted a small group with a camera trying to film an interview. And over everyone loomed the presence of heavily armed soldiers. We were, I knew, all at their mercy.

*Ya*Ziana leant over and whispered to me, her voice barely audible above the noise of the crowded bus. "Don't tell anyone your real name or where you're from. From now on, your name is Sundi and I am Bijoux."

I nodded before returning my attention to the street.

Finally, the bus was ready to leave. By now it was packed with people of every age and size, as well as goats and chickens, crates with vegetables. What horrors had all these people endured that had forced them to escape? What were their stories? Living in the camp for so long had made my world so small; for the first time now I realised that other people in the DRC were living other kinds of nightmares.

The engine roared to life and we were off, each changing scene indicating another mile behind us, so much faster than walking. Relief washed over me. Even though the air in the bus was thick with dust, diesel fumes and the odours of passengers and animals, I found I could at last breathe easier.

We are on our way to South Africa, to build freedom. Yes, I was really here.

*Ya*Ziana had fallen asleep beside me, cradling our precious fish in her lap. Looking at her face I wondered: Would she betray me again if it was necessary? I had to remind myself of the hundreds of times she had protected me during our capture, how much she had sacrificed for my sake. Even before the rebels attacked our village, she had cared for me as if I was her own child.

No, she was still my sister and my anchor. She hadn't had a choice.

I returned my gaze to the window. Lush green fields stretched into the distance, dotted with clusters of trees and patches of colourful wildflowers. I could see mountains on the horizon. The sun bathed everything in a warm golden glow.

When my eyes started feeling heavy, I rested my head against my sister's shoulder.

18

We drove for days, making several stops along the way. Faces changed as passengers came and went, but the bus always remained packed – when all the seats were filled, people simply sat on the floor. As time passed, the stench of people travelling in the heat became almost unbearable.

Arriving in Kongolo was an immense relief.

The town wasn't as large as Kisangani, but it was just as busy. By now we had finished our food and were again utterly destitute, but we needed to get to Lubumbashi, a city on the border with Zambia four hundred and fifty kilometres to the south. Our only option was, once again, to walk.

As we began down the road on foot, *Ya*Ziana addressed a man wearing a green suit and pointed shoes who appeared to be going the same way.

"Excuse me, sir," she said. "Can you please tell me how far Lubumbashi is from here?"

"Take your dirty hands off me!" the man retorted without stopping.

From the shadows, a woman appeared and gestured to us.

"Are you going to Lubumbashi?" she whispered.

There was a scar on her forehead. Three children – two boys and a girl – peered out from behind her dress. The girl appeared to be the youngest. With her sad eyes, dirty dress and worn sandals, she looked like she was carrying the weight of the world on her little shoulders.

*Ya*Ziana tightened her grip on my hand and urged me to walk on. But the woman chased after us.

"Please, I beg you!" she pleaded. "It's not safe for us to travel alone. I have food and water; I'll share it with you." With a trembling hand, she opened her bag, revealing her meagre supplies. "I just want to take my children somewhere safe."

*Ya*Ziana peered at the woman sceptically. "Do you know how long it will take us to walk to Lubumbashi?"

"It should take about seven days," the woman replied. "But with the children, probably longer."

*Ya*Ziana digested the information, then nodded. "My name is Bijoux, and this is my sister, Sundi."

"I'm Clarisse," the woman replied. "My daughter is Sandra, and my boys are Joel and Jija."

We formed a little group and Clarisse led the way.

As we reached Kongolo's outskirts, we spotted a woman slumped beneath a tree and we hurried over to her.

The woman was badly injured. Her expensive-looking dress and once-beautiful headpiece were stained with blood. *Ya*Ziana and Clarisse tried to resuscitate her, but it was too late. The woman slipped away before our eyes. For a while, we just stood there, feeling a strange sense of loss, though we didn't even know her name.

*Ya*Ziana was the one who broke the silence. "Help me carry her body so we can bury her."

Together we lifted the woman's lifeless form and carried her into the forest. While *Ya*Ziana and Clarisse dug a shallow grave, we children gathered stones to cover it.

When we were finished, we stood around the grave in silence. None of us knew anything about this woman – her name, where she came from, whether she had family, or the circumstances that led to her abandonment and death. Would anyone be looking for her? What we did know was that her apparent privilege hadn't saved her from suffering so many women's fate.

*

We have been walking for a few days when Jija falls ill with stomach cramps and diarrhoea. Our pace slows significantly.

"It must've been the water," Clarisse says in distress. "He says he drank from a pond."

We must drink from the rivers we pass, but it's always a gamble. Yesterday Jija went looking for fruit and told us when he returned that he'd found a pond.

"You should never drink water that doesn't flow!" Clarisse had scolded. But there was nothing she could do about it then. Nothing but pray.

Now he is pale and he can barely stand on his feet.

Clarisse is in tears. "We can't go on – I must find help. Jija needs medicine. I have to look for a village."

With heavy hearts we wave goodbye to Clarisse and her children, wish them well.

YaZiana and I are on our own again. To get to South Africa, we need to push on to Lubumbashi.

*

In the days that followed, we crossed paths with several other travellers from different countries, each with their own stories and struggles. But gradually they disappeared, leaving us with only the trees for company amid the vast expanse of forest.

Day in and day out. Walking and walking.

Hoping we were still going in the right direction.

"Are you hungry?" *YaZiana* asked, glancing over her shoulder.

"Me?" I replied, pointing at myself.

"No, Popina, I'm talking to the tree behind you."

"What kind of a question is that? Of course I'm hungry! I can't even remember the last time we ate."

YaZiana just looked at me blankly. "Can you please hurry? We need to get to the base of the next mountain before it gets too dark."

We trudged on in silence and I started to feel bad about shouting at my sister.

"I'm scared, *yaya*," I confessed. "How can we know that things will really be better in South Africa?"

"It will be," *YaZiana* said confidently. "The DRC, its people, its beauty, its many resources – it's all been ravaged by war. Like a magnificent animal tied up in a cage. There's nothing for us here."

She looked at me, and her expression softened.

"South Africa is safe. You can go to school. We may even get to see the ocean!"

"What's the ocean?"

"The ocean is like a never-ending river, blue stretching as far as the eye can see. White waves crash against the beach – that's where the water reaches land. The ocean's waves never stop moving to an endless powerful rhythm."

I had never heard this before.

"In the ocean," she continued, "there are creatures of all shapes and sizes, from tiny, brightly coloured fish to whales the size of a herd of elephants. And the sound – it's like music to the soul."

"How do you know all this?" I asked excitedly. "Where did you see it?"

"I've seen pictures in magazines, and I saw it on television when I was still living with Mama," she explained. "You were just a baby."

I remembered *Ya*Ziana's stories about television, but I'd never seen one.

"I want to see it too! But in real life, not television."

*Ya*Ziana laughed – a happy moment.

After that we lost track of how many sunsets we witnessed as we trekked from mountain to mountain, crossing valley after valley.

*

*Ya*Ziana is talking to herself: "We are going to South Africa, we are going to South Africa, we are going to South Africa …"

Maybe there is no South Africa, I think. *Maybe we should go back.*

I feel like we are walking in an unreality of circles, circles, circles. There are no animals, no sounds, just walking, walking, walking. Maybe we are walking on the same spot and the forest is moving around us.

"… we are going to South Africa, we are going to South Africa …"

Can somebody please help us?

"… we are going to South Africa, we are going to South Africa …"

Mama Nisodin, if you can see us, why are you not doing anything?

"… we are going to South Africa, we are going to South Africa …"
My sister saved me.
"… we are going to South Africa, we are going to South Africa …"
My sister is scaring me.
"… we are going to South Africa, we are going to South Africa …"
My sister is killing me.
Now we are both seeing dead people.
I don't know if I can survive this.

*

"We're going to die, *Ya*Ziana! *Die!*" I couldn't control my emotions any longer. The exhaustion, hunger, thirst, fear – it had all become too much. And doubt had crept into my mind; our plan, our dream had started to lose its clarity.

The journey seemed to have the opposite effect on *Ya*Ziana: she was at times devoid of emotion. Her face these days was hollow, her hair patchy as we again fell into starvation.

I leant against a tree. "*Yaya*, I can't carry on."

"We are almost there. I need you to be strong." Her voice was firm. "Just imagine your first day in a classroom, with your very own books and crayons. You'll learn how to read and write …"

But the thought of school couldn't console me, and I broke down in tears.

"I miss home, our village, playing by the river. Why can't we just die? That would be much easier than this."

*Ya*Ziana tried to pull me closer, but I pushed her away.

"Nisodin has abandoned us!" My voice choked.

"Listen, *popi*," she said more gently. "This walk is nothing compared to what you will achieve, my little sister. The world is waiting for you! They need to hear your story. This isn't about me or you, or even about us. This is about the lives you are going to change."

I continued to sob.

"Look at me," *Ya*Ziana persevered. "You remember the woman I have told you about in my dreams? It's *you*, Popina." Her eyes lit up with conviction. "*You're* the one who is going to inspire people. This walk is just a test. Now come on – we're not far from Lubumbashi."

"No. There's no point in all this walking. It's better to die."

I could see that *Ya*Ziana was taken aback. Then her expression changed.

"Fine! Stay! But do me a favour. Make it a quick death. Don't torture yourself." She shoved the gun she still carried into my folded arms. "Shoot yourself in the head. Make it quick. But I refuse to be a coward."

And she turned from me and walked away.

I sat down, tears still streaming down my face, feeling the cold, heavy weight of the gun in my trembling hands.

I waited for my tears to subside so that I could see what I was doing. What difference would a few minutes make? No one would know I was dead, and no one would care.

I don't know how long I sat there with the weapon in my hand.

Finally, I raised the gun, pointing the barrel towards my head. My finger tightened around the trigger.

The scream that escaped from my lips tore through the silence of the forest; the birds around me flurried in panic.

Not today, whispered the voice.

I lowered the gun.

How was it that, no matter how dark things were, this voice always managed to ignite a spark in me? Somehow it gave me strength even when lifting my head was too much effort.

Slowly, I got up and walked in the direction in which my sister had disappeared.

"*Ya*Ziana! *Ya*Ziana!" But the only sound was my own voice echoing through the stillness. I picked up the pace, panic rising. "*Ya*Ziana!"

And then there she was, seated under a tree, her face wet.

I knew she had never intended to desert me. I rushed to her, and we hugged each other tightly, our tears mingling as we cried.

19

When we finally reached Lubumbashi it was roughly four months since we'd escaped from the rebel camp. It felt as if the whole city was vibrating – the busyness and chaos were overwhelming. Litter was scattered everywhere, buildings were damaged, there were too many vehicles and people moving about too fast.

Holding my sister's hand, I looked at all the disorder. *Ya*Ziana had told me that Lubumbashi, the second-largest city in the DRC, also used to be the cleanest. Now, after decades of conflict had forced thousands of people to flee their villages, it was dense and overcrowded.

"Don't let go of my hand," *Ya*Ziana said urgently. "We need to find transport to Zambia."

We made our way through the crowded streets, weaving through throngs of people and vehicles. *Ya*Ziana spotted a woman wearing a brightly coloured dress standing rocking a baby beside a Toyota pickup truck. She looked kind. Every now and again she smiled at the baby.

"Excuse me." *Ya*Ziana and I approached the woman. "We're looking for transport to Zambia. Do you perhaps know if this pickup is heading there?"

The woman greeted us warmly.

"You're in luck – we are from Zambia," she said in French. "My husband and I just came to deliver and load new stock, then we're heading back home to Lusaka."

*Ya*Ziana was fluent in French and quick to reply.

"If there's space once we have loaded, you can sit in the back," the woman offered. "Do you have passports?"

"No," *Ya*Ziana replied cautiously.

The woman just nodded. "What are your names?"

"I'm Bijoux, and this is my little sister, Sundi."

"My name is Lucie." The woman opened the passenger door and took out a bottle of water and a piece of bread. "Here you go – you're welcome to sit in the back so long and eat. I will tell my husband you need a ride to Zambia."

We gratefully accepted and settled onto the back of the pickup, savouring this stranger's food and kindness.

"*Bonjour*, Bijoux, Sundi," a male voice said a little later. Lucie's husband had the same inviting smile as his wife. He started loading boxes but ensured there was enough space for us to sit comfortably. A few moments later he got into the driver's seat and turned on the engine.

Soon we were at the Zambian border. There the soldiers appeared to know Lucie's husband, and allowed us to pass without incident.

We had just left the DRC.

*

Whenever we stopped over the hours-long drive to Zambia's capital, Lucie checked on us and gave us more food and water – a stark contrast to the previous leg of our journey. And, as we passed through the changing landscape, *Ya*Ziana again spoke to me about the importance of school.

"It's vital for a woman to be independent," she urged. "And education is key to independence. Only those who go to school can eat and be respected, so in South Africa you must learn all that you can. Let your school desk be a place of joy – a reminder of the few children who have the privilege to be educated."

I flushed with excitement – imagine being part of such an elite group! I felt a profound sense of purpose. I knew exactly what I needed to do in this new season in South Africa. In my heart, I truly believed the promise that education would unlock my freedom – and a brighter tomorrow.

"But also, never forget where you came from," *Ya*Ziana added. "Remembering your roots is what will keep you motivated. It will enable you to appreciate every book, every lesson, every small step of progress in South Africa …"

In Lusaka, Lucie's husband arranged for us to travel to Harare, the capital of neighbouring Zimbabwe, by bus. He also gave us money to give to the soldiers at the border so that we could continue our journey. With immense gratitude, we bid our guardian angels farewell and boarded the bus.

Travelling to Harare, Zimbabwe's diverse scenery had us in awe. Unlike the DRC, in which months of walking had taken us through hills and valleys of endless green and misty forest, we now found ourselves staring through the bus window at sprawling savannas that changed into dense bush and back again. We saw all kinds of wildlife and passed villages with colourful markets, hives of activity along the sides of the road.

In Harare, for the first time in my life, I saw skyscrapers and modern buildings. From my seat in the bus I had to crane my neck to take it all in, but the heights were almost too much for me to process. Outside the window the streets buzzed, alive with the rhythm of everyday life.

But when we disembarked, it was once again just *Ya*Ziana and me.

"Where to now, *yaya*?" I asked as we surveyed the throngs of people.

"Now we need to find a way to South Africa," she replied, scanning the crowds.

Suddenly she stopped – she'd overheard someone mentioning South Africa. She turned and approached a group of people.

"We are trying to get to South Africa. Can you please help us?" she asked in Swahili.

"Where are you coming from?" asked one of the men. He had short, curly hair and kind eyes.

"We come from Congo," *Ya*Ziana replied.

"We are from Ethiopia and we are going to South Africa. You can join our group," the man offered.

*Ya*Ziana was elated and we immediately fell in with the Ethiopians, who started moving away from the bus terminal. The first man was already explaining the rules.

"Don't ask anyone their story. We won't ask questions either. Just follow and try to keep up." His tone was serious but not unfriendly. "And no names. You can call me +251." It was the dialling code for Ethiopia. He indicated *Ya*Ziana and me. "You're from the DRC, so you can be +243 and the little one is just 243. That's how you must introduce yourselves. Understood?"

We nodded obediently.

"Remember, if anyone stops you and asks anything about where you're from, what happened to you or where you're going, say nothing," he repeated. "We can't wait for anyone who falls behind, so you must keep up. It's vital that we all cooperate and work together – it's a long way." He handed *Ya*Ziana a bottle of water.

Then the man called +251 guided us to the outskirts of Harare and into the bush beyond.

*

Over the next few weeks we slept in the bush, in forests and, as we moved further south, on farms. When we found ourselves on a maize farm, we took lots of mielies to eat on our journey, and sometimes we were able to find cabbages and spinach near to where we slept.

The Ethiopian called +251 proved to be a good person and a strong leader – another member of the army of well-doers that made our escape possible and bearable. When he saw me battling to keep up with the others, he would lift me onto his back, sometimes carrying me for hours. When we passed occasional wildflowers, he would pick a few and hand them to me.

We felt safe in the group because there were also other women. Unlike us, they had prepared for the journey, but +251 always made sure *Ya*Ziana and I had enough to eat and drink. The rest of the group cared for us, and addressing one another in number codes somehow lent a sense of camaraderie and belonging.

We were about halfway to the South African border when we came across a group of Zimbabweans who warned us that the border controls had become very strict.

"If you try to cross to South Africa there, you run a great risk of being sent back to wherever you came from," they warned. They suggested that we enter the country through Mozambique instead.

And so we changed our course east to Mozambique. And walked for many more days.

*

We reach the border with Mozambique one bright afternoon.

Our leader orders us to rest – he says we must wait until dark to reduce the risk of being seen. He and another man leave for a few hours to look for a place to cross. We all understand the gravity of the situation, and the wait is tense.

When it is dark, +251 leads us to the border fence. In fearful silence we climb through a hole he has made, and walk till dawn.

Over the next four days we walk some of the way, and catch lifts when we can on trucks carrying coconuts. We have no food left now so we eat the coconuts too.

Our safe arrival in Maputo brings immense relief, but our stay is short. Only one more border before we enter South Africa.

2006–2007

Johannesburg, South Africa

20

The border at night is a different world – shadows stretch long under the dim moonlight and the air is thick with whispered fears and quiet prayers. Some have prayed all day, prayers of desperation to carry us through.

Are there armed guards lurking in the darkness?

One man climbs through the hole he's dug under the fence and then *Ya*Ziana goes through, and then +251 passes me over the fence to the first man. The man hands me to *Ya*Ziana and she puts me on her back.

I clutch at breath as we inch forward, each step a delicate balance between hope and terror. Around me, the others move forward in silence, their faces tight. A single misstep on the dry earth is deafening, every rustle of fabric a potential betrayal. My heart pounds as we cross – will they call us back? Will a shout break the silence?

But then we are far enough away. A rush of cool night air fills my lungs, and for the first time in months, I feel something close to freedom.

We are on South African soil – the realisation is almost too wonderful to bear.

This is freedom. We have made it.

*

Getting across the most feared border fuelled me and *Ya*Ziana with renewed determination. We said goodbye to most of the Ethiopians, who had different plans and goals, and secured a lift with +251 to Johannesburg.

Ahead, the road stretched into the unknown.

What will Johannesburg be like? For months I had pictured it as I remembered our village – just bigger, with lots more mango trees, children playing, happy people. Could this paradise really become our new home? I couldn't remember the last time I felt so free, so full of joy.

As the vehicle sped along the highway, I gazed at Johannesburg's cityscape, my excitement overwhelming. We had arrived in our land of milk and honey, of safety and sustenance – a new home where *YaZiana* and I would make memories with our future families. I saw the towering buildings and I imagined the miracle of running water and electricity, imagined myself walking down clean streets filled with well-dressed people on their way to dignified work. I imagined feeding my hungry mind, sitting in a classroom, learning about all the many things I was still yet to discover.

And I truly believed that the hardest part of our journey was behind us.

*

"And so, we are here," +251 declared as our lift pulled up outside Johannesburg's Park Station.

I wanted to shout out loud: "We've made it!"

Instead, standing on a pavement in this strange city, I looked around. I looked at the tall buildings, the fast cars, heard the noise. There was hooting and the smell of engines, people shouting, a train.

There was graffiti on the walls. Plastic bottles and dirty food wrappers littered the ground.

This can't be the place. Where are we?

People were weirdly dressed. I recognised Muslim people by their clothes, but white people were a shock – what had happened to their skin? I stared at blonde hair – "Look at that, *yaya*! The head is gold!"

"Relax, relax, Popina."

But where were the smart buildings and the schools? Where was the promised safety?

I started feeling uneasy, uncertain. Next to me, *YaZiana* was staring around her in shock. No, there was something wrong with this country – a feeling of chaos, even though people weren't shooting each other. And not everyone looked like they had respectable jobs and comfortable homes.

I felt a rising wave of panic. *Where do we go now? Who should we talk to? Where are we going to find something to eat?* Interrupting my thoughts, +251 announced that it was time to part ways.

"No! Please help us! Where do we go from here?" *Ya*Ziana's voice was high with anxiety.

But +251's response was not what we would have hoped for.

"I'm sorry, that wasn't part of our agreement." His words left me stunned, as if he had just slapped me in the face. Then he knelt down in front of me and stroked what was left of my hair.

"Stay brave, little one," he said. "And don't fret. We'll meet again – even if it's in the next life. I'm not leaving you forever."

And then he was gone. Forever.

The abandonment instantly brought up a memory of my father – from the first and only time he ever came to visit me. He had come to collect our vegetables.

*

*Ya*Ziana and I are living in the village, and I am very young. My father is tall and slender, and he moves with confidence in his impeccably tailored suit.

I touch his face – his skin is smooth and dark, in contrast to his crisp white shirt. Even to my baby-eyes he is distinguished, elegant, poised. When he speaks, his voice is deep and calm.

He is my first love.

I beg him not to leave me in the village, to take me with him. He promises that he will always be by my side. Comforted, I fall asleep in his arms, believing.

But when I wake up, he is gone.

My first love – and my first heartbreak.

*

The man called +251 had vanished.

We had not thought we would need to learn how to survive South

Africa. But the truth was that Johannesburg was a bigger, busier place than anywhere I had been in my life, and there was no one to ask for help because no one spoke our language – or any of the languages *YaZiana* knew. We'd thought they would.

Instead, the people rushing around us didn't even seem to notice us.

I wanted to scream. Did they know what was happening? Were they even aware of the suffering in the DRC? And in Sudan, Somalia, Burundi?

Would they believe us if we told them?

At a loss, we walked inside the station – into the huge space, below a roof that soared above our heads like the highest tree canopy. So many people. So many voices, languages, smells and different styles of clothing. Talking, talking into cellphones.

So many new things. We found an escalator, and we must have gone up and down for half an hour or more. Exhilarating! I couldn't understand why no one seemed to be enjoying it as much as we were.

Then we wandered around looking at the stands where vendors were selling clothing, cosmetics, toys. There were dolls that looked like dead people. They were for children, *YaZiana* explained, and I wondered why people would sell such scary things to children.

A food stall displayed fresh fruit. We hadn't bought food in the village – food was everywhere, in the garden, in the forest – and I was used to helping myself. I went to pick up an apple off the table but *YaZiana* slapped my hand away and frowned – "Popina, no! You must pay!" So fruit wasn't free here, even though I was hungry. And even though the fruit was right there in front of me. Next to that, the smell of freshly cooked meat reminded me of more we couldn't have. We were starving, but we had no money.

We kept on walking and we found a public toilet. In the village we'd had holes in the ground – this toilet was so flashy. Mesmerised, I opened the tap and watched the water flow. And then I drank. And drank. And drank. Tap water – a small miracle.

With nothing else to do, we sat down on a bench and watched the ebb and flow of people, each with their own destinations, their own stories. Buses painted in bright colours came and went. People got on and got off, a blur of motion and colour.

I had no idea who these people were or where they were going, but I found myself thinking that all these people were also on a journey, that every departure and arrival was a piece in a bigger picture. Were these people also running, like us? Chasing after dreams, fleeing from nightmares?

"We're in South Africa now," *Ya*Ziana said after a while.

"Yes, we are – there's no fighting here."

"So you know what you're going to do?"

"Yes, *yaya* – I am going to school, just like you told me. No boys and no drugs."

As evening approached, the lights of the station flickered on over the thinning crowds. *Ya*Ziana suggested we lock ourselves in the public toilets. It wasn't ideal, but it seemed our only option.

And it would surely be just for the night.

*

The toilet stall in which we lived for the next few weeks was dimly lit and the smell of disinfectant barely masked more potent odours. I would stay locked in the cubicle the whole day, looking at peeling paint and cracked tiles, while *Ya*Ziana went to look for food and whatever other help she could find.

Every day while I waited for her, I listened to the sounds of the station: the muffled announcements over loudspeakers, the hurried shuffle of feet, snippets of arguments and conversations, occasional laughter – the only indication of the world beyond my toilet cubicle. A reminder of the freedom we had fought so hard for, but that seemed out of our reach.

A knock on the stall door startled me.

"*Vula kunini uhleli lana ez itoilet?*" a female voice asked. I didn't understand the language but I could sense that whoever was knocking was impatient.

I froze, my heart racing. What was she saying? What did she want? I had no idea how to respond, or if I should respond at all. So I just kept quiet, trying my best not to move.

The woman went into the stall next to mine, climbed onto the toilet seat and peered over the dividing wall. I stole a glance up at her and saw that she was old. She gestured towards the door.

"*Vula, vula umnyango,*" she said, this time with a more sympathetic tone.

I realised she wanted me to unlock the door. But *Ya*Ziana had given strict instructions not to open for anyone. The woman appeared to be desperate, but *Ya*Ziana had been adamant. I didn't know what to do.

The woman climbed back down, walked to the front of my stall and knocked on the door again. With a deep breath, I decided to take the chance. I unlatched the lock and quickly moved backwards to the corner of the stall, pressing my back against the cold tiles. I watched the woman intently. What could she possibly want from me?

She tried to come closer but I squirmed.

"It's okay, *ntombazana, bendifuna uku nika ukutya* – I just want to give you some food," she said in a soft voice, and continued talking in her strange language.

I sensed that she was worried about me.

"*Uphi umama wakho?* Where is your mother?"

I knew what "mama" meant, but when I still didn't respond, she reached out and offered me a lunchbox filled with rice and chicken. I grabbed it and started eating.

A group of people came into the bathroom, their loud chatter suddenly filling the small space. Sensing my anxiety, the old woman moved closer into the stall and gently closed the door behind her. Now she was inside the stall with me.

She touched my arm. "My name is Mama Cindy."

Her voice was comforting. She pointed a finger at herself and said, "Cin-dy." She did this three times, emphasising each syllable.

"My name is Ma-ma Cin-dy," she said again.

I realised she was trying to tell me her name, but I was more interested in the food, which I was shoving into my mouth as fast as I could, scared she might take back the lunchbox. I hardly chewed before swallowing.

Mama Cindy was in her late fifties. Her short curly hair was speckled with grey. She wore a simple, well-worn dress that hugged her plump figure and an apron marked with evidence of her daily chores. Her eyes were kind. But her radiating smile was her most striking feature.

Mama Cindy handed me a bottle of water. The ice-cold bottle surprised me so much I almost dropped it. How many years since I'd drunk ice-cold water! I removed the cap and gulped. It was gloriously fresh.

After I had licked the remnants from the lunchbox, Mama Cindy gently took it from me and gestured for me to stand outside the stall while she fetched a caddy with some supplies. I realised she wanted to clean.

As she scrubbed the tiles and wiped down the surfaces, my mind raced. Should I tell *Ya*Ziana that I had opened the door for someone? Or should this be the one and only secret I kept from my sister? In the end, I decided I wouldn't tell her. I was sure she'd be angry.

When Mama Cindy was finished wiping down the stall, she gestured for me to go back inside. As I did, she gave me a gentle hug.

"I'll see you *kusasa*, tomorrow," she said.

Her words may have been foreign, but I realised that I had made a friend. She was kind, she gave me food and water, and she cleaned the toilet. For the first time in a long while, I felt a sense of comfort.

*

*Ya*Ziana would usually return in the evenings shortly after Mama Cindy had left for home. She mostly brought back uncooked food like cabbage or some carrots or tomatoes that had been discarded by market vendors. On lucky days she would return with bread, and on rare occasions chicken or sausage.

On sunny days *Ya*Ziana would take me to sit outside, and we would watch the buses arriving and departing, the people getting onto and out of them, walking into and out of the station, from one platform to the next. We sat in the centre as if caught in a vacuum, with life moving all around us. And still we couldn't leave the station.

Sometimes I wondered how things would have turned out if Lola had been with us. Would she have survived the walk across the DRC? Or perhaps we would have never even escaped.

One day when we were sitting on one of the station benches, I noticed fresh blood stains on *Ya*Ziana's dress. When I pointed at them, she just kept quiet. I looked up at her face and saw that it was bruised. I looked at her for a long time. I didn't have the energy or perhaps the courage to ask, and she didn't offer to explain. But I knew what had likely happened to her, and she knew that I knew.

No, life in South Africa was nothing like we'd thought it would be. Apart from Mama Cindy, no one offered help, no one reached out to us. The most frustrating part was that we couldn't communicate because we didn't know the languages.

"Nisodin will provide," I said to my sister, gently touching her bruised face.

*

More weeks passed, and still we lived in the toilets at Park Station.

The only joy and hope in my life were Mama Cindy's daily visits. She never failed me, and I guarded my secret closely, always fearful that *Ya*Ziana would find out about her. Sometimes I would keep some of Mama Cindy's food for *Ya*Ziana – I would tell her that someone had given it to me when I'd left the toilet stall to drink water at the basin. The lie felt heavy, but protecting my sister from worry felt more important than telling the truth.

21

Another day. At least *Ya*Ziana now allowed me to sit outside by myself, a welcome break from the cramped and cold toilet stall. The sun was shining, but it felt like our dream of building freedom was disintegrating with every passing day. Would we ever get out of here? Would we ever feel safe and comfortable again?

As I sat there on a station bench, *Ya*Ziana arrived with a tall, handsome man. He had a well-groomed beard and was fashionably dressed in jeans, a white shirt, stylish sneakers and gold chains around his neck.

She introduced him as Patrick, and told me we were going to leave with him.

I didn't know what she was doing – as far as I was concerned, all men were a no-no. But she told me he had promised to help us.

"I have a place where you can stay and be safe," he said with his broad smile. I couldn't believe what I was hearing because he was speaking our language, Lingala! Putting his hand on *Ya*Ziana's shoulder, he promised he would help my sister find a job, teach us both English and enrol me in school. He wanted to make sure we were alright, he said, because we were from Zaire.

*Ya*Ziana seemed relieved. This was everything we had hoped for – our first real prospect of escaping Park Station in weeks. I could see that my sister had been won over, and how could I blame her? She was the one who had tirelessly scoured the streets looking for scraps of a future for us. I just felt that something was wrong – I wasn't convinced we could trust this man. But I had to listen to my big sister.

*Ya*Ziana told me to gather our belongings – two plastic bags with some food we'd stored, Lola's hijab and the warm clothes we'd carried all the way from the DRC. I decided to push my fears to the back of my mind.

It was natural to feel distrustful – so many men had failed us – but this might be different. After all, he spoke Lingala.

As we started to follow Patrick, I looked behind me, hoping to catch a glimpse of Mama Cindy.

But Patrick seemed in a hurry.

*

Patrick's car was deep metallic green that glistened in the sunlight. Inside, it was spacious, and even though I could see it wasn't new, it was clean and comfortable. I felt like a VIP sitting in that car – the second one I'd ever been in.

As we left Park Station, I looked through the window at the changing city. Skyscrapers sparkled in the distance, reflecting the late-afternoon sun. The car moved smoothly through the bustling streets and soon we entered a quiet suburb with high walls and large gates that gave glimpses of beautiful, well-maintained houses.

A tall gate opened and he drove up to a house that looked to me like a mansion. He welcomed us warmly and led us inside to a table in a large, modern kitchen. We eagerly accepted the meal he offered – rice and beef stew, simple food that was comfortingly familiar. Just what we needed to lift our spirits.

When we had finished eating, Patrick handed me a cold bottle of Coca-Cola. I'd never seen or tasted Coca-Cola before, and the fizzy sweetness exploded on my tongue, unlike anything I had ever savoured. While I sat alone at the table drinking my cooldrink, *Ya*Ziana and Patrick sat on the couch and chatted. I watched them out of the corner of my eye, slowly sipping my Coke, not wanting to finish it too quickly.

I still had a bit of my bottle left when I started to feel dizzy. *Ya*Ziana's voice was fading in and out – and even though she and Patrick were still sitting on the couch nearby, she sounded distant and muffled. The next thing I knew, my vision became blurred. The room around me seemed to spin.

I tried to call out to *Ya*Ziana, but no sound came out of my mouth.
I realised something was terribly wrong.

*

It feels like just moments later that I wake up in a cage – a cage surrounded by other locked cages, cages filled with girls like me.

Girls are crying or making desperate noises, their voices echoing off cold, damp walls. They look dizzy or drunk, their eyes glazed with fear.

Nothing makes any sense.

*Ya*Ziana is in another cage with older girls.

We appear to be in an underground room without any windows.

Where are our bags?

*

It wasn't long before I learnt how Patrick earned his living. He went around bus stations, parks and airports, luring destitute women and girls with promises of food and safety, only to sell their bodies to other men. The girls were from different countries – places like Zimbabwe and Ethiopia, and there were also white girls. Some of the girls had been there for a very long time.

*Ya*Ziana and I had escaped from a rebel camp, pushed our minds and bodies to the limit in a trek on foot from Central Africa, persevered and defeated the odds time after time – only to find ourselves here.

Same story, different place.

I wanted to cry but I didn't have any tears left. What was the point anyway? I felt utterly empty.

Patrick had men working for him who acted like guards. They gave us food and water three times a day. There was a toilet, but we were only allowed to use it at certain times. We had to force ourselves to use the toilet during those times because they wouldn't open the cage in between.

Most days they would come for a "round", as they called it. They made us bath using a bucket and then dress up. When we were clean and looking decent, they gave us injections in our arms.

When they injected me, a sense of calm washed over me. I felt completely relaxed. My current reality seemed to disappear, and I imagined myself back in the village, playing with my friends, even those who had long since died.

Even though the injections blurred my vision, I could see well-dressed men walking around the cages, picking their prey. The men mostly wanted the younger girls, the smallest ones.

So my cage was one of the most popular.

*

It was only a matter of time before I was chosen.

The tall guard with the tattoos on his neck, who everyone called "Four", was the one who came to fetch me. He took me upstairs to a bedroom. Four's every movement was deliberate, authoritative. He wore a gun tucked into the back of his jeans. He told me to sit on the bed.

From what I could see through my spinning vision, the room was neat and clean. I noticed an old man coming towards me. His skin was pale, almost translucent, and his hair was white. Had he been here when we'd come in? He took off his clothes, pushed me down onto the bed and got on top of me.

Physically, I was too weak to resist. In my mind I was in the village, running around with Lola, alive and happy.

The man took my hand and instructed me to start rubbing his privates. I didn't cry, I didn't scream – in fact, I didn't feel anything. Every now and again I heard the man say things like "Good girl" and "Wow, you're so obedient, my sweetheart." But it was as if he was talking to someone else.

Eventually, he wanted to be inside me. His breathing was laboured and loud, and it echoed against the walls of the quiet room. Sometimes he paused as if to gather his strength, then he'd take a few breaths and continue. My gaze was fixed on the chandelier with its sparkling lights. I had never seen anything so shiny – so close, yet out of my reach.

But no emotion stirred within me. It felt as if my spirit had left my body, or perhaps it had simply retreated somewhere. I was a hollow vessel. In the world where I played with Lola, I felt alive. But in this world I was barely conscious.

I expected the man to be violent and aggressive like all the others had been. Instead, he was gentle. He kept on calling me his sweetheart. After he was finished, he offered to run me a bath – my first time in a bathtub. The warm water was soothing, and the bubbles smelt of sweet flowers. Sinking into the water, I felt peace.

By the time I got out of the bath, the man had ordered some food. He placed before me a generous portion of tender meat and vibrant greens. I stared at it in astonishment.

As I was finishing my meal, there was a knock on the door. The sound echoed through the room, disturbing the temporary calm. Four entered and abruptly told the man his time was up. The old man nodded solemnly.

As I made my way back to the basement, I saw several other men emerging from rooms along the corridor.

*

It wasn't long before even this life became routine. And at times I felt it was an improvement – at least we had regular meals and less violence. But it was very, very far from the life we had intended to build for ourselves in South Africa.

The old man became a regular and I learnt that his name was Johan. Whenever he booked a session with me, he'd bring me dolls, gifts and food. At the time he seemed like the kindest person I knew, despite the distorted nature of our relationship.

But sometimes I would wake up in the morning and notice scars, things going on with my body that I couldn't recall. And I remember that I started feeling there must be something wrong with me that I kept getting into situations where I was abused by men.

Why am I going through all of this?

I started feeling that I was not supposed to be here, perhaps I should never have been born, there was a mistake somewhere. I wished so badly I could die. I wished I could just drop dead.

To create an illusion of normalcy, the guards sometimes allowed us small girls – aged four, five, and me, eleven maybe, and small for my age – to play outside. There were lots of really young girls there – the younger you were, the more they wanted you. But we weren't really playing – we couldn't any more. We were like statues. And the gate would open sometimes, and no one would run.

One day when we were playing outside, I noticed that the gate to the street had been left open. I looked around but there were no guards. Had they just quickly stepped inside? Were they watching us from the house? Perhaps something had happened elsewhere on the property, and they'd thought it was safe to leave us alone.

Suddenly, the voice in my ear: *Run.*

A trick of the wind?

I can't run – they'll kill me!

I looked at the other girls – had they noticed the open gate? It seemed not, and it was perhaps in that moment that I realised true freedom is not only the absence of physical constraints. *Ya*Ziana and I had come to this country to build freedom, and to do that I had to defy internal barriers too.

The voice this time was louder: *Run!*

But where would I go? Here I had enough to eat, I had Johan. I knew what to expect. As awful as the situation was, it had become a twisted kind of security. The injections they gave me brought me peace and relief, and I had come to hunger for them. I realised with a sickening feeling that I was reluctant to escape. The outside world was terrifyingly unknown.

Even louder than before: *RUN!*

Without another second's hesitation, my feet just started running.

Don't look back, instructed the voice.

*

Despite my drugged state, it is as if I am running with supernatural strength. Something has overtaken me, propelling my feet. I start screaming, begging anyone who can hear me for help.

I can hear the guards running behind me. I keep going.

I have done this before.

The houses lining the street have neat lawns and vibrant flowerbeds. It is quiet, except for the guards shouting behind me. The sky is dark with the threat of rain. But I keep going, my bare feet slapping painfully against the smooth pavement. Despite it, I run and run. Once or twice I see someone peek out from behind a curtain or from the safety of their patio, faces curious, concerned. No one helps, but as more people start to notice me, the guards stop and let me go.

I run into a narrow alleyway between two houses. The high walls are covered with ivy, perfect for hiding. I crouch among the shadows, try to catch my breath.

I listen intently for any sounds – the guards might be trying to trick me. But I can only hear birds and the distant sound of traffic.

22

A car hooting, but far away. Then another, closer, followed by the sound of screeching tyres. I rubbed my eyes and opened them slowly. A tiny patch of pale sky visible between the high-rise buildings. In my limbs and down my spine, I could feel the all-too-familiar stiffness after a night spent on concrete.

Initially after my escape from the house, I hadn't been able to sleep at all. Every sound and movement had startled me. I hadn't known where I was but I had started roaming the streets of Johannesburg. I was one of the kids you see in the streets collecting food in the bins, asking people for money, for food. Futureless. I had walked and walked, navigating the maze of cold, concrete structures, relying on my instincts to stay safe.

The fatigue had eventually got to me, and whenever I could finally find a protected piece of pavement, I had somehow started managing to fall asleep, even if it was restless and marred by nightmares.

The hunger was the worst. Relentless, it gnawed at me, leaving me no choice but to beg. I approached strangers, my voice a whisper, asking for anything they could spare. Some days I scavenged through bins. On the worst days, I stole. I justified it to myself: *It's just a loaf of bread; the owner is not going to die.*

But whenever a kind soul offered me a coin, I refused it. Where I came from, money was evil. Those with money were the ones who raped children. I couldn't accept.

The loneliness was overwhelming at times – I missed my sister – but loneliness was more comfortable than my fear of strangers.

*

As one day blurred into another, I started noticing that I wasn't well. My skin was clammy, my hands would tremble, and waves of dizziness would wash over me, making it hard for me to stay upright. I knew what my body needed and it wasn't food.

My craving for the injections became all-consuming, suffocating the need for food, for shelter, for the breakthrough that would bring me to freedom. I fantasised about them. I could almost feel the needle piercing my skin, the relief.

I eventually decided to return to the house, though I now had no idea where it was. My need was stronger than any fear of what would happen if I returned.

I had only just started walking when something brought me to a standstill. At first it was subtle – a faint, painful yearning. But before I knew it, it had grown into an overwhelming sense of sadness and loss – and I broke down and cried, right there on some random street corner.

The tears flowed without end. I cried for my sister, for Lola. I cried for everything and everyone I had left behind, wondering if they were dead or if they had managed to escape. I cried for my village, my home. I cried for all the pain and the loss I had suffered and the pain those I loved had suffered. I simply surrendered to the despair, succumbing to a feeling of utter helplessness.

Crouching down on the pavement, another wave of dizziness hit. Everything started spinning. I felt light, as if I was floating. I tried to steady myself, but my body betrayed me. The edges of my vision darkened.

The last thing I felt was the cold pavement against my cheek.

23

The smell hits me first – later I will know it as the smell of medical antiseptic.

Slowly, I open my eyes.

I am in a bed, but it's not like any bed I've seen before. It's very high off the ground, with metal railings. Everything around me is white: the bedding, the walls, the curtains. Next to me some kind of machine is making strange beeping sounds. I can hear low voices but I can't see anyone.

How did I get here?

When I try to move, I find there is a tube in my nose.

A tall woman in a white uniform comes in, dark hair pulled back in a tight bun. She is smiling but her body has the same alien smell as the room. She puts her hand on my arm and starts talking, but her voice is just a jumble of sounds.

Nothing makes sense, and absolutely nothing is familiar.

Have I died? Is this the afterlife?

A wave of panic – this is absolutely terrifying. I try to get out from the covers, pull at the pipe in my nose, scream, "*Ya*Ziana! *Ya*Ziana!"

The woman tries to calm me, pushes me back into the bed. She's trying not to hurt me but her composure in this weird place makes me frantic. The more she talks, the more I fight back, desperate to get away from this place. I am talking in Lingala now, going crazy.

She injects me and I fall asleep.

I wake up and it happens again. Now I manage to break free and I get to the door and through it into a long, bright passage with shining floors. I start to run. People are sitting in chairs all the way down – some injured, covered in blood-stained bandages, some sick and wrapped in blankets. They all stare.

A woman is shouting, running after me, joined by more women in white uniforms, their footsteps echoing loudly down the corridor.

They grab me, pull me to the ground, hold me down. Another needle. I think it's the same as the injections at Patrick's brothel and I want to thank them, but then the world starts to fade.

Every time I wake up, I panic and they put me back to sleep.

*

Warmth on my shoulder. A hand. Someone was whispering softly.

I didn't recognise the words, but the voice was soothing. Opening my eyes I saw a blurred face. I blinked until the face came into focus.

It was a woman. She had pale white skin and long red hair. Her eyes were kind. Her one hand was on my shoulder; the other rested on a book. I was in the same white room as before. When I tried to sit up, she gently pushed me back onto the pillows. Then she reached for a glass of water that was standing on the cabinet next to the bed and offered it to me.

Not taking her eyes off me, she tilted her head slightly towards the door and called out for something or someone. Again, the fear of being in the afterlife.

Where am I? Who is this woman? Why am I in this bed? Where is my sister?

The same woman from before entered the room holding a plate of food. Okay, this was something. Beside her was a tall black man with a white coat and a file in his hands. The woman set down the plate while the man approached my bed, flipping through the pages of the file.

I could sense that the man was in a position of authority and I somehow understood that he was here to help, but I didn't trust any man at this point. Even though he had a neat appearance, and seemed compassionate, I felt a deep-seated fear.

He turned to the woman in white and the red-haired woman and addressed them. While she was listening to him, the red-haired woman picked up the plate and tried to feed me, but I was too scared to eat and started mumbling in Lingala. I barely knew what I was saying – but hearing my language might somehow validate my existence.

And then there was Lola, sitting on the edge of the bed. So perhaps I was dead after all.

"How are you?" she asked, her voice gentle as a lullaby and her eyes glowing.

I just stared at her.

"Everything's going to be okay. You're safe now," she said. But then she dropped her gaze and said she had to leave and that I wouldn't see her again.

I struggled to grasp her words. "Where are you going?" I asked.

"I'm going to my mother."

And then she was gone, and my brief joy dissolved as the man's voice pulled me from my hallucination.

"My name is Dr Kongolo. Where in Zaire do you come from?" he asked in Lingala.

He understood me? He was Congolese! But Patrick had also claimed to be from the DRC. I just stared at the doctor, too scared to move. No, I thought, I was not going to fall into that trap again. I was going to keep quiet until someone found my sister.

Dr Kongolo introduced the two women: the red-haired woman was Eve and the other was a nurse named Lucinda. They both smiled at me. Without waiting for any response from me, he explained that it was Eve who had found me on the streets, nearly lifeless, and brought me to this place, this hospital. He pulled up a chair and sat down, placing the file on his lap.

The background noises of the hospital – monitors beeping, voices and shuffling footsteps on linoleum – seemed very loud. Looking at the two women I felt slightly comforted – they both seemed genuinely sympathetic.

When Dr Kongolo asked for my name, I hesitated. But then I glanced at Eve and Lucinda.

"My name is Popina."

"It's nice to meet you, Popina." He said he had noticed the scars on my body and that my blood tests showed there were drugs in my system.

"What? Drugs?" I said.

His expression turned grave. "Heroin. It's poison. You've been poisoning your body."

"No, no, it wasn't me! Four is the one who injected me."

"Who is Four?"

And so, I recounted my story. Everything, from being captured by rebels and living in their camp to how my sister and I had escaped, walked across the DRC and arrived in South Africa. I explained about Park Station and Patrick's house and what had happened there. As I spoke, Dr Kongolo translated for Eve and Lucinda, and by the time I had finished their faces were wet with tears.

"It will do you good if you eat something," Eve nudged.

Looking at the plate of food, I realised I was actually very hungry. After I had finished every last crumb, Dr Kongolo handed me some medicine.

"This will help you sleep," he said. "You deserve some rest."

*

Dr Kongolo returned the next day accompanied by police officers. He explained that they were going to try to find my sister, and that I needed to provide as much information as possible.

The presence of policemen with guns was terrifying. I realised that I was now in a position to save *Ya*Ziana, but I didn't know the neighbourhood where Patrick's house was, and I had no idea how to get there. Apart from Four, I didn't know the names of any of the men who worked for Patrick.

My sister, I knew, had the courage of a lion. Her strength had carried us all the way from captivity to South Africa. She had kept me going throughout our journey, making sure I was safe and providing for us as much as she could. She had made unthinkable sacrifices to ensure we arrived. As I tried to remember anything I could about Patrick's house, I kept thinking, *YaZiana needs me.*

By the time the policemen left I was exhausted. But the possibility of being reunited with my sister had ignited some hope. Before, when I had fallen asleep in the hospital, a part of me had wished I would never wake up again. Now I wanted to be well-rested for when I saw *YaZiana* again.

*

Eve visited me every day. She brought extra food and dolls for me to play with. Sometimes she bathed me, giving me beautiful dresses and bright-coloured socks to put on. Occasionally she would read to me. Our languages remained foreign to one another, yet it felt like we shared an understanding. I had meanwhile learnt from Dr Kongolo that Eve was American, and a devoted Christian who worked tirelessly for the Salvation Army.

One day Eve arranged with Dr Kongolo to take me on an outing. It was a Saturday morning and she came early to bathe me and then helped me get dressed in a bright-red dress she had brought, accompanied by white stockings and black shoes. She even put a white Alice band on my head.

We went to a play park. The weather was perfect – the sky was bright blue, the sunshine warm on my skin. There were so many fun things to play on – swings, slides, merry-go-rounds – and I tried everything. We laughed and ate sweets. I couldn't remember when last I had felt such pure happiness.

When we returned to the hospital, Dr Kongolo, a few police officers and some people I hadn't seen before were waiting. I discovered that the strangers were social workers and they wanted to speak to Eve. While they talked, I sat cross-legged on my bed, clutching my dolls and absentmindedly tracing the hems of their clothes.

Everyone looked very serious. The only thing I could think was: *Please don't take Eve away.* After what felt like a lifetime the group seemed to relax, and then they were all shaking hands and smiling. When Dr Kongolo approached me, he looked relieved.

"We have good news for you, Popina. You won't have to stay in the hospital much longer. Eve is going to find you a new home where you'll be safe and have enough food to eat, and where there are many other children to play with."

I couldn't believe what I was hearing. I had to stop myself from hugging him.

"Is that okay with you?" he asked carefully.

"Yes!" I replied.

"Eve must just fill in a few forms to promise us she will take good care of you. And then it is settled." He reached into his front coat pocket and pulled out a small piece of paper. "Popina, if you ever feel unsafe, call me on this number."

The symbols on the card meant nothing to me – I had no idea what it said. But it didn't matter. I had learnt to trust Dr Kongolo. It felt like a dream come true, except for one thing.

"Doctor?" I said. "My sister?"

He looked down for a moment.

"We haven't been able to find her yet. But the police are still looking."

*

As it turned out, Eve was in the process of relocating from Johannesburg to Port Elizabeth, and she had requested that I be put in a children's home close by so that she could keep an eye on me. That's how I would end up in a children's home in a small Afrikaans town called Despatch, on the outskirts of what was then called Port Elizabeth, a two-day train journey from Johannesburg.

The morning of our departure she arrived at the hospital early to help me get ready. By now I had learnt a few words of English, so we could communicate a bit better, but I sensed that she was worried. I was worried too. It felt like I was about to go on a great adventure, but what lay ahead was completely unknown.

And of course I was thinking about *YaZiana*. Was she still at Patrick's place? Was she alright? Something inside told me she was still alive – I could sense it – but my heart wasn't at peace. I was afraid of moving further away from her, of losing her or never seeing her again. At the same time, I knew our story had not come to an end and that I was getting closer to my mission. I had never forgotten what I was here to do – my sister had repeated it so often, made sure it had stuck in my head. I had come to South Africa to study, to read and write and count and learn languages. To be the best student I could be.

This time I returned to Park Station beautifully dressed in new clothes, holding Eve's hand and a suitcase of brand-new belongings, and by the time we stepped onto the train my excitement had largely taken over my trepidation. The vibration of the engine, the smell of the tracks, the smooth hum as the train started moving forward – it was thrilling.

*

The train clicks over its tracks, a gentle rhythm. But as I sit staring out of the window, still holding tightly onto Eve's hand, my tears begin to flow. I cry because I am happy, because my path has crossed with caring people, and because it is starting to feel like I have a future.

But I also cry for what I have seen and for those who never managed to escape the DRC. It makes no sense to me why I am here when so many others have been left behind. The guilt twists inside me. Yet I also know there is no point in feeling guilty.

I will have to make my survival count.

I will have to tell my story for the sake of all the children I saw die. Who else will tell the world of their pain and their loss? Who else will give them a voice?

The train's steady movement carries along the lost children's stories like ghosts.

*

Inside the train, the worn seats and faint smell of leather gave the impression of something old but comfortable. Outside the window, dusty fields were giving way to green hills. Eve still had her arm around me but appeared to be lost in her own world.

The food they brought us was simple – sandwiches and fruit. I barely ate. The knots in my stomach were growing tighter.

As night fell, the dim interior lights cast long shadows across the cabin. The world outside the window faded to darkness, interrupted only by the occasional flicker. I huddled closer to Eve, wrapping myself in the small blanket the train had provided for us.

Sleep didn't come easily. Too many thoughts – about the past, about whatever might lie ahead. Sometime in the night I spotted a lone star twinkling in the sky. I imagined it was guiding me, a tiny beacon of hope on this uncertain journey.

2007–2010

Despatch, South Africa

24

"We're going to arrive soon."

As dawn finally broke, Eve squeezed my hand in encouragement.

Pulling into this town called Port Elizabeth, the sky was overcast and a soft drizzle tickled the window – but in the distance lay a glimmering ocean and an endless blue horizon. I got up from my seat and pressed my face against the window.

You were right, YaZiana.

It was exactly how she had described it: a blue expanse with no end in sight. If only she were here to share this moment with me.

The train station was an old and weathered brick building. Eve had explained to me that a social worker named Samantha would be meeting us, and I spotted her even before Eve did. She looked serious and business-like, but she had a kind smile.

There were a lot of formalities to get through, and Samantha accompanied us first to a hospital for me to have some standard health checks. That was followed by what felt like an endless amount of paperwork at different institutions. The visit I was most anxious about was to the Department of Home Affairs because Eve had explained I would be registered as an "illegal alien". It was a great comfort to have her by my side through it all. She made sure I wasn't hungry or thirsty, and that I took my medications on time.

As we moved from place to place, my thoughts kept drifting to *YaZiana's* words: *When we get to South Africa, focus on education. Learn to read and write – that's how you'll find your purpose. But never forget where you come from and those you have left behind.*

Finally it was time for us to go to Oosterland Youth Centre. I felt an immense sense of relief as we pulled up at a beautiful children's home.

The centre was made up of a number of individual houses, all with crisp white walls. In between the large houses were well-kept lawns and garden beds full of flowers and greenery. Children were playing around outside – when we entered the main building I could hear them laughing.

The home's social workers showed me around the common areas and then took me to the house where I would be staying – House Esther. Each house had its own name, displayed above the front door. At the door I met my house mother, Tannie Santana, her husband and their two children. Tannie Santana told me that there were eleven other girls living at House Esther – I would be the twelfth.

I had never dreamt I would have a home again, and the house was unlike anything I had ever been in. It was a large double-storey with a living room downstairs, with a television and a computer, a dining room and a kitchen with a fridge filled with food. At the bottom of the stairs was a bookshelf crowded with books. Alongside that was Tannie Santana's personal living rooms and bedrooms for her family.

The only other home I had ever known was the small hut in the village where I had last lived with *Ya*Ziana seven years before. Every time my sister and I had reached a new milestone on our long journey, every time we'd miraculously avoided another danger or survived to find another meal – every one of those times I had yearned for a home.

They took me upstairs where there were five bedrooms and two spotless bathrooms – one with a bath and one with a shower. Some of the upstairs bedrooms were shared, but I had been given a room to myself – my very own bedroom.

"Welcome to your bedroom," Eve said with a smile.

I froze at the door. This was beyond what I could comprehend, and yet here was a private and safe space, with my own bed, my own cupboard.

I had walked all the way from Central Africa to find myself with my own bedroom in a children's home in a small Afrikaans town.

It felt like a completely different world.

*

"See what happens when you don't give up?"

It was a few days after my arrival and I was talking to my reflection in the mirror. I smoothed out my new blue school dress and slipped on the matching jersey. Excitement welled in my chest. *You'll go to school in South Africa* – Ya Ziana had planted this promise in my heart, even when it had felt impossible. And now here I was, wearing a school uniform for the very first time.

As I looked down at my spotless socks and polished shoes, I couldn't help but think of Lola. Of running barefoot on the dusty roads of our village, climbing trees, our feet caked in dirt. Now here I was, stepping into a world neither of us could ever have imagined.

I glanced up at the ceiling of my room.

"Lola, please be with me today." And it did feel as though I was carrying her spirit.

In my new school bag I had packed a lunchbox with a bottle of water and two slices of bread with peanut butter and jam – yes, that had become my favourite since I'd first tasted it at House Esther. I couldn't get enough of it, especially with a warm cup of milky tea – small joys that were beginning to displace past hardships.

"*Is jy gereed?*" A beautiful girl called Bianca burst into my room and handed me a new blue hairband. Although I couldn't speak a word of Afrikaans yet – and could hardly speak English – I understood the warmth behind her gesture.

When the bell rang for breakfast, Bianca and I walked downstairs together and found the other girls already seated at the breakfast table, all seemingly eager to see me dressed up in my new school uniform. They showered me with compliments. They said I looked beautiful.

*

Susannah Fourie Primary School is just a few streets away from the children's home, and it is much, much bigger than I ever imagined a school to be. When the car pulls up at the entrance I am sitting in the back with Samantha and Eve, and Eve is holding my hand.

Nerves flutter in my chest. *This is it*, I tell myself, and my mind races. *Will my teacher be kind? Will I learn to write today? Will I even be able to do this?*

I clutch Eve's hand, uncertainty gnawing at me.

I have left everything I know – all for the chance to sit at a school desk.

Eve reaches into her handbag and pulls out a pink diary with my name printed on it and a matching pen. Tools to shape my future.

*

Up until I was twelve years old I had never even seen a school, a classroom or a desk. I couldn't read or write, and I had never even met or spoken to a schoolteacher. I was so far behind that I should really have started right at the beginning in grade one, but they had decided to place me with others my age in grade six.

We first went to see the principal – a tall white man with a grey beard – who handed me a sweet. Then he walked me, together with Eve and a few teachers, down squeaky-clean hallways to my classroom. Everything seemed so bright, and the air seemed to hum. My heart raced faster with every step.

My grade-six classroom was light and cheerful, with posters covering the walls. Meeting my teacher, Mrs Ferreira, I felt starstruck. And I never imagined my teacher would be a white person! She had short brown hair, a very pointy nose, and was tall and thin. When she took my hand, she smelt like flowers.

Mrs Ferreira led me to my desk – and what a relief it was to finally see it! It was made of wood, just as I had imagined, and on it were crayons and a pile of books covered in bright paper – all waiting for me. I just wished *YaZiana* could see that I had made it – *I am in a classroom! I have a teacher! I have pencils! I have books!* I felt so alive and I understood then why I hadn't died before this moment.

As I stood there at my school desk, tears began to stream down my face.

"Can I help?" asked Mrs Ferreira.

"*Alekho, alekho*! School, school!" was all I could say.

The other children in the classroom couldn't understand why I was crying and admiring my desk. They just laughed – "*Wat 'n kind is dié, Jevrou?*" What kind of child is this? – but I couldn't stop my tears. I knew this was what I had come here for, what I'd fought so hard for.

This desk.

What a privilege it was to be able to go to school every day. What a privilege to be taught! What a privilege to be cared for in ways I had never thought possible.

The teachers and Eve knew what that moment meant to me, even if the children didn't. The adults gathered around me, held me and cried with me.

25

As much as I was excited about being in school, for the first few weeks I felt isolated and different – a weird-looking girl with a big head, patchy hair and a distended stomach.

I battled to do the most basic things. I couldn't even hold a pencil – I barely knew what a pencil was. My classmates would giggle and whisper as I fumbled, and eventually they just laughed outright. I felt the sting. My face burnt with shame as I tried to steady my hand, blinking back tears as the blackboard words blurred.

Because I lived in an Afrikaans children's home, I had been put in the Afrikaans stream – the only black child in an all-white class. I'd come from a place where I'd never seen a white person, so the idea that I might be treated differently because of my skin colour had never even crossed my mind. One girl, Nadine – who was tall, with long blonde hair – seemed to take particular pleasure in teasing me. One day she pointed at my head and said, "Your hair looks like an old scrubbing sponge. Do you even wash it?" Her words sent her group of friends into fits of laughter. Then she sneered: "Your skin is dirty. Someone should wash you with bleach."

I stood there wishing I could disappear. After that, Nadine and her friends' taunts followed me like shadows and replayed in my head even when I wasn't at school. I would sit quietly in the passage of House Esther fighting back tears, wondering if I would ever belong. As it turned out, I didn't fit in among the black students in the English stream, either. They called me *kwerekwere* – foreigner.

At the same time, though, something inside me began to stir: a determination to prove them all wrong, to show them that my appearance and vastly different background had nothing to do with my value and potential. I was determined not to be the girl who struggled to hold a pencil. I would do whatever it took.

But it was still early days and for now there were times when the pain of being ostracised was unbearable. During break I would slip away and hide in the girls' toilet, locking myself into the last stall just as I had in Park Station, and sitting on the cold tiled floor. That became my sanctuary, a place where I could grieve my losses in silence, away from those who seemed intent on tearing me apart.

Sitting alone, nibbling on my sandwich, I would think of Mama Cindy. I would close my eyes and imagine her speaking to me, her words comforting as a blanket.

Each tear I shed in those first few weeks in Despatch felt like a release of something tightly wound. Deep down I knew that this pain wouldn't last forever and I held on to the belief that things would get better, that one day I would find my sister and my place. I may have been hiding in the girls' toilet, but I knew my story wasn't over.

*

One day I heard a voice at the cubicle door.

"You know," it said gently, "eventually you'll have to be brave and face everyone. Then you can enjoy your break time. You can't hide in here forever."

I was silent, hoping whoever it was would go away. But instead there was a knock. More irritating, light, rhythmic taps. Knock. Knock. Knock.

"I'm not leaving till you open up," the voice said cheerfully.

"*Los my uit*! Leave me alone!" I snapped in my newly acquired Afrikaans. But the knocking didn't stop.

"Come on, you'll feel so much better," the voice urged.

Finally I got up and unlatched the door, opening it just enough to see who was bothering me.

Outside stood a petite girl with straight black hair parted neatly to the side, not a strand out of place. Her school uniform was impeccable. Her almond-shaped eyes, framed by thick lashes, sparkled.

"Hi!" she said. "I'm Anthea."

I blinked, unsure of how to respond.

"It's okay," she said softly, holding out her hand.

Reluctantly, I opened the door a little wider and shook her hand. "Hi," I whispered.

Anthea's face lit up. "There you go! Now you don't have to eat alone any more."

Her gentle tug pulled me out of the toilet towards the playground, where she found a place for us to sit and finish our lunch.

For the first time since my first day here, I could appreciate where I had found myself. The play area was a wide open field with lush green grass that bore faint traces of dampness from the recent rains. White lines crisscrossed the ground, marking the boundaries for various sports. Clusters of boys dominated different parts of the field – one group kicking around a soccer ball while another group played rugby. Most of the girls sat under two gigantic trees, oblivious to the boys' energetic games.

Trrrrrrrrrrring! When the bell echoed across the playground, Anthea reached for my hand and pulled me back to our classroom. At that moment, a vivid memory of Lola washed over me. I had made a friend.

As I came in from break, my teacher caught my eye and gestured for me to come to her desk.

"Yes, Mrs Ferreira?"

She looked at me, her gaze steady, then pointed a finger at my hands.

"What are those, Popina?" Her voice was gentle but firm.

I hesitated for a moment. "Hands."

She didn't break her gaze, then pointed at my eyes. "And what are those?"

"Eyes, ma'am," I replied, feeling a little unsure of myself.

"And you can use your hands and see with your eyes, right?" I nodded. "And can you walk, Popina? Are your legs working?"

I believed I had already proved that. "Yes, ma'am, I can walk," I answered.

"And can you think for yourself? Is your brain working?"

That made me shrink. I lowered my gaze. "Yes, ma'am."

She paused for a moment, then lifted my chin with her finger.

"Aha," she said softly. "We don't look down when people talk to us, Popina. We look up, with confidence."

I straightened my posture and met her gaze.

"Never allow yourself to be treated as lowly, Popina. You are as strong, clever, capable and beautiful as anyone else in this room."

Her words washed over me and I realised that she must have noticed the children's treatment of me.

"Anthea, come here," she summoned my new friend. "If any children bully Popina, I want you to let me know, okay?"

Anthea nodded and slipped her hand into mine.

I mattered.

*

As the weeks passed by, I immersed myself in this unfamiliar way of life and grew more accustomed to the people and routines of school and the children's home. For the first six months, Mrs Ferreira stayed after school and met me on weekends to give me extra support and encouragement. She was the kind of teacher who didn't just teach lessons from books; she taught from the heart and reminded me that I could accomplish anything I set my mind to.

I had realised early on that everything would fall into place if I could communicate. Since I was in an Afrikaans children's home and an Afrikaans class with English as a first additional language, learning Afrikaans became my top priority.

The children's home got me a translator. They would talk to me in Lingala and translate my classwork back into Afrikaans and English – that started my language journey. At the same time, I was learning to read. In books I would trace letters with my finger, repeating words over and over until they became familiar.

Watching television also helped. At six-thirty, after supper, the girls in House Esther would gather in the living room to watch *7de Laan*, their favourite Afrikaans soapie. At first, I watched just because that's what everyone else was doing, but when I realised the show could teach me the language I started paying close attention. While the characters spoke in Afrikaans, there were English subtitles so I could learn both languages at the same time. Using *7de Laan* as my secret classroom, I repeated words and phrases, mimicked accents and intonations, and slowly but surely I began to understand.

Within six months, I had learnt to speak, write and read Afrikaans and English fluently, and went from being at the bottom of my class to ranking in the top three. I also started doing well at sports. I loved running so I started doing athletics. In my mind I went back to the time when I was running for my life. And I was really good.

Because I loved sports, I would be at school the whole day before returning to the children's home in the early evening. As the months passed, I developed a habit: when I woke up in the morning, I'd look at myself in the mirror and say, "Yeah, *jou oulike ding*, this is the plan, you cute thing: we are going to school today, you're going to do the best that you can. On the sports field you're going to run all those girls out and then you're going to come back, eat your supper and study hard!" That was my schedule every day. And I'd repeat it constantly in my head.

The day I received my first good mark for a test, I caught Nadine looking at me. Her smug smile was gone, replaced with surprise – almost disbelief.

It was the sweetest victory.

26

Sunday morning and I was standing in the hallway of what had become my new home. Through the window I could see the morning sun glistening through the green garden. I loved looking out of the children's home windows, watching the changing light of the day, the cool silver of moonlight at night or raindrops that streamed in patterns down the glass.

The house already held a sense of permanence for me. Walking down the hallway, I paused to admire the framed photos on the walls, the faces of those who had lived here before me. Lola wouldn't have believed how far I had come. Sometimes even I couldn't believe it. And Samantha the social worker still promised to find my sister.

I wandered downstairs to the wooden bookshelf that leant crookedly against the wall. I felt drawn, and gently brushed my fingers across the spines of the books, reading the titles. Reading and writing were no longer just something I dreamt about – it was now a reality.

"Thina, come – we're all waiting for you!" Bianca shouted from outside. Bianca had become my best friend at the home – perhaps because she was just as curious about me as I was about her.

Turning away from the bookshelf I smoothed down the bold red dress I had chosen for the day, along with black sandals with a slight heel. I was a young teenager now, and the click-click sound as I walked made me feel very grown-up.

I loved my new name, Thina. I had chosen it myself, a deliberate step away from the painful weight of being Popina. I needed a fresh start. The name was inspired by Christina Aguilera and Tina Turner, music icons I'd seen on television and had fallen in love with. The name represented everything I wanted to be: strong, vibrant and unafraid to dream.

"C'mon, Thina!"

This morning a few of us from House Esther were going to church together. In her patient way, Tannie Santana had explained to me what church was. She'd described it as a place where people go to talk to God about their struggles and their dreams. I didn't fully understand, but it had sounded like a sacred and comforting place. To practise my reading, I'd been going through an Afrikaans Bible, so I'd read about Jesus. I'd started talking to Him, but in a strange way I felt like He already knew me and that I knew Him.

The home's minibus idled outside, its engine humming softly, and we climbed in one by one, twelve girls, our excited chatter filling the small space. When we arrived at the local Dutch Reformed Church, I stepped out of the bus and gazed up at a spire that reached into the sky.

Inside, the church felt both familiar and strange. The first thing I noticed was that there were only white people here. I took a seat in the pew next to Bianca, grappling with the contrasts between the world I had come from and the one I now occupied. Tannie Santana left us girls to settle and went to sit with her own family.

The service started with singing. I didn't know the words and couldn't sing along, but I was aware of a presence surrounding me, something bigger than all of us. When the singing ended, the pastor began the sermon, his voice echoing above the faint rustling of people paging through their prayer books. Even though I could by now understand most of what he was saying, I concentrated on absorbing the moment.

Then people started forming a line at the front, and the pastor handed them pieces of bread and what looked like red grape juice in a cup. I knew the juice had something to do with Jesus's blood, and I immediately sensed that this was sacred and meaningful. I wanted to be part of that, so I joined the line behind Bianca.

I had just taken a piece of bread and sipped the juice when she grabbed me by the arm.

"No, Thina! You're not allowed to take that!" she exclaimed in panic.

The church grew silent; everyone was staring at me. Why wasn't I allowed to do this? Tannie Santana came hurrying down the aisle, her face crimson. Turning to the congregation, she began apologising in Afrikaans – "*So jammer*, I am terribly sorry. She's new; a foreigner. She doesn't understand what she has done."

The heat rose to my cheeks as what felt like hundreds of pairs of eyes bore into me. My heart pounded; I didn't know where to look or what to say.

Summoning all my courage, I finally spoke in Afrikaans: "I know this is the blood of Jesus. Jesus's blood is red. Tannie's blood is red. My blood is also red. So, what have I done wrong?" In my mind it was that simple: in God's eyes we were all the same.

My words were met with a stunned silence. Tannie Santana grabbed me firmly by the wrist and commanded me to return to the minibus. Flushed with embarrassment, I started walking to the back of the church.

I was stopped by the pastor, who pulled me into a hug. I think he understood that I had understood. And to my surprise the rest of the congregation followed his lead. One by one, people came forward, offering me a hug or squeezing my hand. The atmosphere shifted and became something extraordinary. Out of nowhere, churchgoers broke into prayer, their voices rising together, creating a protective shield around me. It was a moment of profound connection as everything that divided us fell away.

After that day, the church became deeply involved with the children's home. On our birthdays they would bring us cake, koeksisters and milk tart, along with beautifully wrapped presents. Mostly they gave the gift of acceptance.

27

"You mustn't worry. Just focus on being a good girl at school."

Though the social workers and police had reassured me that they would find her, *Ya*Ziana remained missing.

How could I not worry? How could I focus on being good when every time I closed my eyes I saw my sister's face? Her smile. Her voice. The way she had held my hand as we crossed so many rivers and climbed so many hills. How many times had she told me to keep going, to stay strong? To get myself educated.

The last time I'd seen *Ya*Ziana she was in a cage in the basement of Patrick's brothel, that look of fearlessness in her eyes. I never imagined I'd have to keep going without her.

*

It had been about a year that I'd been in Despatch and I had held on to the social workers' promise like a lifeline. I had convinced myself that they would find my sister. They *had* to find her. But the truth – the raw, aching truth – was that I didn't know if I would ever see *Ya*Ziana again. She seemed to have vanished into thin air, along with the rest of the life I had known.

To relieve my grief, I decided to write to my best friend. But my heart felt heavy, burdened, and the words were slow to come, weighed down by what I couldn't say.

Dear Lola,

Where do I even start when so much has happened? Life hasn't been the same without you.

I can read and write now – can you believe it? It feels strange to write this letter, knowing you were learning to read in the village long before the idea even crossed my mind. I can still see you sitting cross-legged on the floor as Mama Nzembo traces letters in the sand teaching you to read the Quran.

I remember watching you. For me, life was about climbing trees and running races. But you carried quiet hope, a belief in something greater. The rebels destroyed everything we knew and loved, but I'll never forget how you whispered your prayers at night.

*Ya*Ziana and I escaped. Somehow we made it out of that night-mare. I wish you could have too; and I wish that you could see me now. I made it to South Africa. I'm here. And I can write – in three languages!

As we waded through cold rivers and hid from soldiers, *Ya*Ziana told me her dreams. She told me that words build bridges in even the darkest places. Every letter I write now is because of both of you. You showed me that words can be prayers.

I still miss you so much. Every day.

Love,

Thina

I sat back with the pen in my hand, staring at the letter. Had I done enough for Lola? Had I failed her?

"Thina, what are you doing up so early?"

I jumped, but it was only Tannie Santana. She pulled back the heavy curtains, letting soft morning light spill into the dining room. I looked up from my paper, squinting at the light.

"I'm writing a letter to my friend, Lola," I said. "My best friend. I'm trying to understand my feelings about her and my sister."

Tannie looked at the table cluttered with sheets of paper, a dirty teacup from the night before. Fresh coffee was brewing in the kitchen, the aroma drifting through the morning chill. She raised an eyebrow and gave a half smile.

"So young, but so wise." She gave a small sigh and made her way back to the kitchen.

Her words lingered. Perhaps I was no longer just a child who needed to be told what to do – perhaps I was becoming someone with something important to say.

I folded Lola's letter into a tiny square, pressing each crease as if sealing a secret. Holding it tightly, I walked back upstairs. The house was still cloaked in the early-morning quiet. Everyone else was asleep, their soft breaths echoing faintly through the walls. My eyes drifted to the bookshelf against the wall and I brushed my fingers against the spines of the books until I stopped at the one I'd been longing to read: *I Am David* by Anne Holm.

The cover showed a boy walking alone in the snow. I recognised that boy, and my heart ached for him.

28

Every second weekend, all of the children at the children's home were placed with foster families – part of a system designed to give us a sense of belonging and ordinary life. I always spent those weekends with Eve. Being with her allowed me to imagine what it was like to have a family again.

But like all good things in my life, this happy arrangement was not to last. I'll never forget the day Eve came to the children's home to tell me she was leaving. It was a sunny afternoon, but the brightness outside did nothing to calm the storm inside me.

Samantha, Eve and I were sitting in the small living room where she broke the news. Her time in South Africa had come to an end – she had to return to the United States. I stared at her, trying to make sense of her words. It felt like a punch to the chest.

"Why?" I asked, my voice barely a whisper.

Eve reached out to hold my hand.

"I wish I could stay, Thina," she said sadly. "But I really can't."

A familiar ache settled in my chest – sadness mixed with something darker. An overwhelming sense of abandonment. It was as if life had created a cruel pattern just for me: everyone I loved seemed to disappear. Everyone I loved left me, died or went missing. *I must be cursed.*

Eve held me as I cried but nothing could remove the cold fear that I would forever be left behind, forever lose the people who mattered most. When she finally let go, she promised to write, to call, to stay in touch. But I knew it wouldn't be the same, and the thought of another goodbye felt unbearable.

A few days later Eve returned for her last visit. Before she left, she handed me a Bible, its worn cover soft under my fingers.

"Since you can read now," she said. "Remember that Jesus will never abandon you."

I stared at the road long after Eve's car disappeared.

Coming up behind me, Tannie Santana put a reassuring hand on my shoulder. "You are safe with us, Thina."

"And we've managed to find you another foster family," Samantha added. "They're based in a nearby township called Motherwell. It's a Xhosa family. I think you'll do very well there."

*

My first visit with the new foster family was scheduled for the very next weekend.

The minibus carrying me and a few other children drove us to our foster homes on the Friday afternoon. I remember that the sun beat down relentlessly that day. As we entered Motherwell, I was struck by the unfamiliar sights. In Despatch I had become used to seeing mowed lawns, spacious homes, my pristine school with its sprawling sports fields.

This seemed like an entirely different world. The houses were tiny and packed tightly together. Some were made of bricks; others appeared to be assembled from corrugated iron and wooden planks. The walls of some houses were painted in bright colours, but were mostly faded. Laundry lines crisscrossed between the houses; clothes flapped in the hot breeze. Children played barefoot on the dusty streets.

We passed a school with barren grounds. I could see no rugby field or swimming pool – just an expanse of dry gravel with scattered patches of grass littered with paper and plastic. A rusted swing set stood in one corner. Many of the classroom windows were cracked or patched with cardboard. I sat in silence, absorbing the contrast. What would life be like here? I wondered.

The minibus turned a corner and I caught sight of the towering Nelson Mandela Bay Stadium in the distance as we stopped outside a modest home. The minibus door slid open. Warm air rushed inside, thick with the smell of cooking fires and car-exhaust fumes, and the sounds of the bustling township. I stepped out, holding my bag in one hand and a packet of groceries from the children's home in the other.

166

The door of the house opened and out stepped my new foster mom. She was a stout woman, and she moved with a deliberate, slow confidence. Her deep-brown skin glistened and her sharp, piercing eyes seemed to assess every part of me before I even had a chance to speak. Her face, framed by a headscarf tied tightly around her head, was unreadable.

She clapped her hands. "*Wamkhelekile*, Thina – welcome!"

It seemed more of an order than a welcome. Behind her, two older teenage girls came out, their bare feet kicking up small clouds of dust. Both looked at me but said nothing. One had her hair in tight cornrows, while the other's short Afro gave her a slightly softer appearance. They grabbed the grocery bag and started walking back towards the house. The woman looked at the girls and then shifted her gaze back to me, but she didn't move.

As the minibus sped off, I couldn't shake the feeling that I didn't belong here. Still, I followed the girls towards the house, aware of the woman behind me. This wasn't the warm welcome I had hoped for. It was something entirely different, something I couldn't yet name.

Inside, the house was small but very tidy. The lounge was dominated by a huge television – far bigger than the one at the children's home – that sat on a wooden stand, surrounded by family photos and trinkets. There were three bright-red and slightly worn couches. On the wall above the television were framed photos of the two girls. Their faces were younger in the pictures, and they were smiling broadly, arms around each other.

The woman introduced us. The girl with the Afro was Thembi, and the one with the cornrows was Sisipho. They nodded in acknowledgement but didn't say much. My new foster mother continued talking rapidly in isiXhosa. I tried to follow her tone and gestures, but the language was still largely unfamiliar.

Feeling lost, I asked, "Ma'am, could you please speak in English? I don't understand isiXhosa."

Her eyes narrowed, and she crossed her arms.

"No," she said firmly. "You are in my territory now, and you must speak isiXhosa."

My cheeks burnt with embarrassment. I didn't know how to respond. I wanted to explain that I was willing to learn, as I had learnt English and Afrikaans, it's just that I couldn't grasp it overnight. Instead, I stayed quiet, staring at my hands.

"Thembi, *hambani ni yombonisa irum yakhe,*" the woman instructed, waving her hand dismissively. She settled into one of the couches and started rummaging through the groceries I had brought.

I assumed Thembi had been told to show me to my room because she led me down a narrow passage that smelt faintly of dampness and soap. She opened the door to a small room and my eyes widened.

Inside, two double mattresses left barely any other space on the floor. And there were seven girls already inside. Some girls were lying around, half-asleep, while the rest sat in a cluster, paging through old magazines and chatting in low voices.

I hesitated in the doorway, clutching my bag awkwardly. There seemed no room to put it down, let alone unpack. The room felt suffocating, crowded with bodies, blankets and a few scattered belongings.

My heart sank. So, this was my foster family. Eight girls in a tiny, cramped space. I thought of the children's home, where I had my own bed and my peace. Here, there was no such luxury. I desperately wished I could go back.

From the lounge, Mama Thembi – I later learnt that was her name, like her daughter's – raised her voice.

"*Hayibo, iphi inyama apha?*" she yelled.

"She's asking where's the meat," Thembi explained. More shouts, which Thembi translated: "She says she's tired of always getting pilchards and macaroni. She says these packages are absolutely useless."

Humiliation rippled through me. The groceries were meant to help, a token of gratitude for taking me in. I stood silently, unsure of what to do. The other girls paid little attention to Mama Thembi's outburst or to me.

I swallowed hard, fighting back tears.

To distract myself, I reached into my bag and pulled out my book, *I Am David*. I needed to practise my reading anyway – I had promised myself that when I saw *Ya*Ziana again, I would confidently read her any book she wanted to hear.

Scanning the cramped room, I saw a spot slightly away from the chatter. A skinny girl, who looked to be around thirteen, my age, was already sitting there, her elbows resting on her knees as she flipped through a magazine, her wiry frame swallowed by an oversized T-shirt.

"Could you please move over a little?"

She looked up at me, her eyes guarded, but shifted without hesitation. On the cover of her magazine, Beyoncé looked radiant.

"Beyoncé," I said, more to myself than to anyone else.

The girl gave an approving nod before turning her attention back to the magazine.

"My name is Thina," I said.

The skinny girl looked up again, her expression softening.

"I'm Zanele." Then she returned to the glossy pages.

I settled into my corner, opened my book and allowed the words to take me away.

*

Supper was served a few hours later. I stared in disbelief at the plate in front of me. Pap. Just plain pap. At the children's home, supper was always a balanced meal.

Afterwards, hoping to wash off the day's discomfort, I asked where the shower was.

"There is no shower in this house," one of the girls said bluntly. "If you want to bath, you need to use a bucket and boil water for yourself."

I began to understand that cleanliness wasn't a priority in this house and I wasn't prepared for this. At the children's home we always showered after supper, and Friday night meant gathering in front of the TV to watch movies – a time I often used to dive into my books while the others laughed at the screen. Here there was no escape into movies, and studying was impossible. Instead, as the night wore on, random people started streaming into the small house – drinking, laughing and filling the space with noise. I sat clutching my book, longing for the peace and routine I had become used to.

Saturday came. I wasn't interested in exploring the unfamiliar surroundings so I stayed in the cramped room. We were fed only once that day, and it was pap again. But who was I to complain? Going days and weeks without food had been my reality. Where I came from, any food was a luxury. I tried to tell myself that this pap, sweetened with sugar and milk, was not so bad.

Zanele, for reasons I couldn't quite understand, remained by my side all of that day. She was a quiet girl with dark skin, even darker than mine. Her hair was short and her eyes – on the rare occasion they met mine – carried a quiet intensity. She'd been wearing the same faded, oversized clothes since I'd arrived on Friday. Neither of us had showered the entire weekend, and no one seemed to care. We sat together in the corner, two silent figures in a noisy world, she with her nose in the magazines and me buried in my book.

That weekend, I vowed to myself that I would learn to speak isiXhosa fluently. Soon no one could gossip about me in secret – and never again would anyone call me *kwerekwere*.

*

Mama Thembi's foster home I visited every second weekend became less a place of refuge and more a test of endurance.

One day, when Samantha hinted that it might be a good idea for me to live with the family permanently, I realised that I had to speak up – I hadn't told anyone about my experiences in Motherwell. When I had finally gathered the courage, I told Samantha everything. I told her about sleeping in a cramped room with seven other girls, how the groceries I contributed vanished into the household and were never used to prepare meals for me. I described how I often went hungry, surviving on one meal of pap a day. I told her about the noise, the stream of unfamiliar men who filled the house every weekend, drinking alcohol from the afternoon until the early hours of the morning. It was an impossible place to study or even find a moment's peace. I explained how out of place I felt, struggling to navigate the culture and the language. My requests to communicate in English had continued to be met with refusal.

Finally, I confessed: "I don't feel safe there. I'm struggling to keep up with school and to maintain any kind of normal routine." I wanted her to know that I wasn't asking for more than I deserved – but I was asking to be placed somewhere safe.

Samantha was devastated. Although the social workers followed a strict application process for foster families, including visiting foster homes, it was not uncommon for people to abuse the foster-care system.

Samantha immediately launched an investigation, and it turned out that Mama Thembi had been exploiting the system, taking in children purely so she could collect the government grants. She wasn't fostering children out of compassion or a desire to provide a loving home – once the children were under her roof, she showed little interest in their health, education or care.

When the other girls at the children's home heard my story, it was as if they'd been given permission to break their own silence. One by one they began sharing their own experiences – stories of abuse, neglect and exploitation that exposed a system riddled with secrets. A pattern of betrayal had thrived in the shadows.

My friend Bianca's story would strike me the hardest. In the coming months she would leave the children's home, but she would stay in touch. Bianca confided in me how her foster mother, desperate to have a child of her own, had convinced her to fall pregnant with her foster father's child under the guise of helping the family.

"You're giving us a gift we could never have," her foster parents had told her to justify the exploitation.

When Bianca was placed permanently with the family, the social workers did not know she was pregnant. Bianca kept this to herself, fearing
that the truth would only bring more trouble. For months she endured
the abuse in silence. When her condition became obvious, her foster parents painted her as a rebellious teenager who had recklessly fallen pregnant,
leaving Bianca to bear the stigma.

When the baby was born, they took the child as their own and turned
Bianca out of the house. Stripped of her baby and any support, she would
have to fend for herself while her foster parents retained their respectability,
their lies shielding them from accountability.

Bianca would be manipulated, used, silenced and then abandoned.

29

"Thina! Phone call for you!"

As I knelt in the yard polishing my school shoes, Tannie Santana's voice broke through the stillness of the afternoon. This was part of the daily routine: straight after school we had to take off our uniforms, scrub our white school socks and polish our black shoes until they gleamed. Only then could we have lunch. I didn't mind; it gave a sense of order.

A phone call? For me? That didn't happen often. I'd been thinking about the mince-and-cheese macaroni we'd be having for lunch – Wednesdays were my favourite.

I quickly put down my brush, wiped my hands on my skirt and hurried into the house.

The telephone hung on the wall in the passage. In her ocean-blue dress adorned with dolphins, Tannie Santana handed me the receiver, her hand absently twirling her short brown hair, freshly cut from a visit to the salon. I could see the concern etched into her face.

"Hello?"

"Thina, this is Tannie Elna," said the familiar voice of one of the Oosterland social workers. "Can you please come to my office immediately? There's something I need to discuss with you."

In the children's home, being summoned to Tannie Elna's office signalled something important. What could she possibly want to talk to me about? I wondered. I hung up the phone and made my way across to the administration building.

In her office, Tannie Elna was waiting. Her blonde hair framed her face, and her blue eyes locked onto mine as I entered. She greeted me warmly – in contrast with the cool professionalism for which she was known. Most of the children found her detached and unyielding, a social worker who prioritised rules over relationships. But I had sensed another side of her – a deep compassion and fierce commitment to every case she handled.

She approached her work with intensity. In her presence, I always felt both nervous and strangely safe.

"Good afternoon, Thina. How are you? Please, sit down." She pointed to the chair opposite her.

"It's going well, thank you, Tannie," I replied formally, my trembling hands giving away my nervousness.

"Thina, I have good news and bad news for you," she began, her expression turning serious. "Let's start with the good news, shall we? We asked the police to help find your sister, *Ya*Ziana. On Monday we received a phone call from Johannesburg. They have found a woman from the DRC on the streets. She says her name is Ziana, and her description matches what you gave us. She also mentioned having a little sister who is lost in Johannesburg. They believe she could be your sister, but we need you to confirm if it's really her. Right now she's under the care of the police. Can we give them a call? Do you feel comfortable speaking to her?"

Her words crashed into me like a tidal wave.

Could it really be *Ya*Ziana? After three years? I nodded slowly, trying to suppress the anticipation and fear bubbling inside me.

My throat was suddenly bone-dry.

"Yes, Tannie, I will speak to her," I managed, my voice barely above a whisper.

Tannie Elna gave me a reassuring smile, picked up the phone and started dialling. I held my breath. Every second felt like an eternity.

When the phone was answered she introduced herself. "Hello, this is Mevrou Pienaar of the Oosterland Youth Centre in Despatch," she told the officer. After a brief exchange, she handed me the receiver. "They've put the girl on the line."

Trembling, I took the phone.

"*Ya*Ziana?"

"Popina?" The voice on the phone was faint but unmistakable.

My heart stopped.

"*Ya*Ziana?" I whispered, tears already in my eyes.

"Yes, it's me!" she exclaimed in Lingala, her voice breaking with emotion. "Is it really you, my little *popi*?"

A sob escaped my lips and I nodded vigorously, even though she couldn't see me.

"It's me. It's really me," I replied as tears started flowing freely.

"Oh, Popina, I've been searching for you for so long! I didn't know if I would ever find you!" *Ya*Ziana's voice was thick with emotion.

"*Yaya*, I thought I'd lost you forever," I cried. "Where have you been? Are you okay?"

She began telling me about her journey – how she had escaped Patrick's house, the challenges she had faced on the streets of Johannesburg and the moment she'd been picked up by the police – each word stitching together the torn pieces of my heart.

"I'm safe now," she assured me, her voice soft but steady. "But I need to see you, Popina. I need to hold you and know this is real."

"Tannie" – I turned to Tannie Elna, who was watching me – "can I go see her? Please! I need to see her."

Tannie Elna nodded. "We'll arrange a visit. I need to speak to the social workers and the police to organise it."

I turned back to the phone, where my sister was still talking: "When I get there, Popina, I'll buy you KFC. We'll be together. We'll build a future ..."

After several minutes – far too little – I reluctantly said goodbye to *Ya*Ziana and handed the phone back to Tannie Elna. She continued speaking to the officer, but whatever they said simply swept over me. My body pulsed with joy, fear and overwhelming relief. I had imagined my reunion with *Ya*Ziana for so many years – but on the phone the words I had practised had simply vanished. Now my mind started racing with all the things I would share with my sister: the battles I had fought and won, the milestones I'd achieved. I was in high school now, grade nine, and I could read and write in two languages. I wanted to tell her about the children's home, about how I had my own room and how, for the first time, I felt like I belonged somewhere. So much had happened in the years we'd been apart – so many moments that had shaped me into who I now was.

It was as if our brief conversation had rewound time because suddenly I felt like a little girl again, clutching my sister's hand as we navigated an uncertain world. I also realised that I hadn't truly processed the journey we had taken, together and each alone, and what it had meant. In the three years since my arrival in Despatch I'd been running on autopilot, moving from one challenge to the next, trying just to survive. But hearing my sister's voice had brought so many emotions rushing to the surface. The pain of our separation, the joy of finding her again, the weight of everything I had endured – it was overwhelming. I wanted to tell her how often I cried myself to sleep but woke in the morning determined to be stronger. How I often felt like giving up but always found the strength to keep going.

But for now all that mattered was that we had found each other. The rest would come. This was her moment, our moment. I made a silent promise to myself that when I saw her in person, I would first tell her how much I had missed her, how much I loved her and how she was the reason I had never stopped fighting. And I would listen to her story because I knew it was just as important as mine.

Tannie Elna handed me a tissue, and it was only then that I realised she'd finished her conversation and put down the phone.

"Now are you ready for the bad news, Thina?" she asked gently.

I kept quiet, clutching the tissue in my hand. I wasn't sure if I could handle anything else at this point. But I nodded.

She chose her words carefully. "This is not easy news to share, and given the circumstances I'm almost certain you won't be pleased with the idea. But it's something we have to discuss."

She paused and looked at me cautiously.

"Thina, we've found another foster home for you. It's with a Congolese family in Port Elizabeth. We believe it will be a good environment for your growth, allowing you to reconnect with your roots and your culture."

I stiffened. Since Motherwell, I'd been placed with several other foster families. But I had raised my voice every time I was mistreated, so they had kept moving me from one family to another. They must have worked very hard to find me a Congolese family.

"Tannie, you know how I feel about foster homes." I tried my best to keep the disappointment out of my voice. "I'm happy here. I don't want to be placed in any other home."

Tannie Elna sighed. I could see she was sympathetic.

"We understand how you feel, Thina, truly. And it means the world to us that you are so happy here. But you must understand, you can't stay here forever. The children's home is a temporary shelter, not a permanent solution."

"But I feel safe here." Desperation crept into my voice. "This is the only home where I don't feel out of place. I have my own space, I don't have to look over my shoulder and my studies are going so well."

Tannie Elna leant forward slightly.

"I hear you, Thina, I do. But we have to think about your future. Part of growing up is learning how to navigate the world outside these walls. You need to learn how to live life beyond the safety of Oosterland."

I tried to swallow the lump in my throat. Her words had struck a painful chord. I knew she wasn't trying to uproot me out of malice, but leaving the children's home felt like losing a lifeline. Life here had its challenges, but it had become my anchor. How could I step into a world I wasn't ready for?

"Your first visit is this weekend," she said. This clearly wasn't up for debate, and the finality of the plans wrapped around me like a cold chain.

"Yes, Tannie." I nodded mechanically but inside I was screaming, pleading for a way out. Showing resistance wouldn't change anything – I knew that much.

As I left her office, the weight of the coming foster weekend bore down on me. Another unfamiliar house, new faces, new rules and new expectations. Would they see me as a person or just another name on their roster? Would they care about me or was I just an obligation? I felt like I'd been thrown into that deep ocean without knowing how to swim.

30

Friday came. I sat in the courtyard of the children's home waiting for my transport to arrive. My bags for the weekend were packed, including the grocery packet, which often felt more like payment than a gesture of care. I tried to stop the whirlwind of questions in my mind, but they kept coming. How would this family receive me? Did they actually want me? Would they treat me like one of their own or as just another responsibility? It was strange how the turmoil was always there, no matter how many times I had gone through this.

The rumble of the minibus interrupted my thoughts. One of the staff waved me over.

This was it. Another new start – a start I wasn't sure I wanted, especially now that I had found my sister. My social worker had explained that I would visit this family every second weekend for three months. If all went well, I'd be placed with them permanently. The thought made my stomach churn.

I got up, adjusted the strap of my shoulder bag and walked heavily towards the minibus. The driver started the engine and we were off. When we had left the premises, I looked back at the Oosterland gates shrinking behind me.

Maybe this would work out. Maybe this family would be different.

*

The first thing that struck me was the neighbourhood. It was a beautiful suburb, unlike anything I had seen before. The house was massive, its polished exterior gleaming in the late-afternoon sun. It was surrounded by a neatly trimmed lawn and flowerbeds bursting with colour. The entire family was waiting for me at the door, their smiles warm and welcoming.

My foster mother, Naomie, stepped forward.

"Welcome, Thina," she said, extending her arms to embrace me.

She introduced me to her husband, Kayi, who nodded approvingly; her step-son, Daniel, who looked to be in his early twenties; her step-daughter, Princess, who seemed shy; and her young daughter, Shekinah, who hugged me tightly and giggled.

Daniel took my bags and led me inside. "I'll show you around," he said with a grin.

He guided me through the house, starting with my room, which was bright and spacious. He set my bags next to my bed, which had been neatly made just for me.

"You'll be sharing the bathroom with Princess, but I think you'll like it here."

The bathroom was pristine and sparkling, with marble countertops and one of the biggest tubs I had ever seen. Then Daniel led me to the balcony.

He gestured towards a set of cosy-looking outdoor furniture arranged neatly in one corner. "This is where I hang out with my friends."

From there, he took me to the lounge. My jaw dropped at the sight of the enormous television. He clearly enjoyed my reaction.

"That's where we all sit and watch movies."

Next to the lounge was a bar area stocked with rows of bottles.

"This area is off limits," he said, looking more serious. "It's only for adults." He lingered for a moment. "Do you drink alcohol?" he asked casually.

I blinked in confusion. "What's alcohol?"

"Never mind," he said with a chuckle. His tone was light, but it didn't ease my apprehension.

As we continued the tour, I tried to take it all in – the grandeur, the warmth of their welcome, the nervous excitement fluttering in my chest.

*

At 5 a.m. on Saturday morning, I was startled awake by Mama Naomie.

"Thina, wake up!" she said from the door of my room.

I rubbed my eyes, disoriented and groggy. Outside the window, the world was still cloaked in darkness.

Without much explanation and in a no-nonsense tone, she began rattling off instructions.

"Today you must wash all the windows on the top floor, clean and tidy up the lounge and do the laundry." She paused. "For dinner I want you to cook lamb and rice for me and the kids, and make pap for Papa Kayi."

I was still trying to process this when she handed me a piece of paper. It was a list of chores that needed to be completed that day, all written in her neat handwriting. I stared at the paper in disbelief, but then I nodded and forced myself out of bed, knowing there was no room to argue or question her demands. I had no choice but to work my way through the list of chores.

I made my bed and slipped into one of my simple play dresses. But I resolved to create a quiet moment in which to focus on my homework, study for a school test and practise my reading. That would be my way of reclaiming my time and staying connected to my dreams.

With this in mind, the chores felt a little lighter. It didn't bother me so much that I had a long list of duties as long as I could carve out some space to focus on me.

And, as it turned out, the family went out for the day, leaving me space to clean the house – it didn't matter how I did it as long as everything was completed by their return. By the end of the day I had managed to squeeze in a little study time. I took a quick bath and then collapsed on my bed, exhausted.

When the family returned later, they woke me up to serve them dinner.

I set the table the way I'd been taught at the children's home and carefully dished up each plate. But it was clear they weren't impressed with my cooking.

"There's room for improvement," Mama Naomie commented.

I wasn't hungry so I excused myself and retreated to my room. As I reached my door, she called out: "Make sure you rest tonight!"

*

Sunday morning came too soon. I woke up to Mama Naomie calling from the hallway.

"Thina, hurry up! You need to be ready in half an hour!"

I quickly got out of bed, got dressed and made my way to the kitchen. Judging by the dishes, the family had already eaten an elaborate breakfast. I found a piece of bread, ate it quickly, and went to meet her in the living room.

Mama Naomie handed me a piece of paper with another list of chores for the day.

"Make sure you do everything on this list. My friend is expecting her house to be spotless when she returns from church."

Before I knew it, I was in the car with Daniel, being driven to a house a few streets away. He didn't say much during the ride, but when he dropped me off, he muttered, "Good luck." There was a hint of mockery in his voice.

The house was just as huge as my foster family's home. As I stepped inside, an older woman looked me up and down.

"You're Thina?"

"Yes, ma'am."

"Well, don't just stand there. The cleaning supplies are in the closet in the kitchen. Get started."

I spent the rest of the morning scrubbing floors, dusting furniture and washing piles of dishes. Each task felt heavier than the last but I pushed through, determined to finish everything on the list. At one point I glanced out the window and saw a group of children playing in the yard next door.

By the time the family returned from church, I had finished all the chores. The older woman looked around, nodding in approval. "You did well," she said.

Daniel came to pick me up shortly after. When we reached the house, I went straight to my room – I couldn't be bothered to eat – and lay down on my bed.

Later that afternoon, I stared out of the minibus window as my transport made its way back to the children's home. The weekend had shifted something in me and I felt strangely calm.

I had resolved to make it work this time, to face the challenge of integrating into the Congolese family. I just had to adapt and persevere. In this case, I at least had my own room and access to the internet, and my foster siblings largely left me alone. I could still focus on studying, finishing school and going to university. If I had to clean the house to earn my keep, so be it.

31

It was a normal Wednesday afternoon and I had just arrived home after a long day at school, my shoulders aching from carrying my heavy bag of books. As I was about to enter the house, Tannie Santana came to the door.

"Thina, there's a surprise for you at Tannie Elna's office," she said excitedly. "Just leave your school bag there – and hurry!"

I froze. A surprise?

I dropped my bag at the door and ran off for the main building, my heart pounding. As I pushed open Tannie Elna's door, my breath caught in my throat.

There, standing in the middle of the room, was *Ya*Ziana.

I ran to her. Or maybe she ran to me. The next thing I knew, we were in each other's arms, clinging like all those other nights. As if letting go now would mean losing each other all over again.

I had imagined this moment a thousand times. What she would look like. Her voice. Was she still the way I remembered her? Would she recognise me after all that had happened in my life, after all that had changed? But no amount of daydreaming could have prepared me for the flood of emotion I felt as our eyes met. Three years melted away – years in which I had grown from a malnourished child into a strong and healthy teenager.

"*Yaya*," I whispered.

Could I believe she was real?

She pulled back just enough to look at me, her hands gripping my arms as if making sure I wouldn't disappear, and my breath caught as I took in her face – familiar yet different. Her features seemed sharper, more grown-up, but her eyes … her eyes were the same. The same deep brown that held echoes of my childhood in the village, of the terrors of the camp, whispers in our tree-cave, the endless valleys and mountains where she would not let me give up. All the things we had seen together and could never unsee.

"Popina, my *popi*. You're here."

Tears blurred my vision. "I'm here. You're here."

She cupped my face with both hands, her fingers tracing my cheeks as if to memorise them all over again. "You – you've changed," she said. "But you're still my little *popi*."

The pain, the struggle, the nights spent yearning, wondering if we would ever see each other again – it all dissolved in that embrace.

Tannie Elna was standing nearby, her hands clasped, tears welling in her eyes that she hastily wiped away.

Lingala tumbled from my mouth. "*Ya*Ziana … are you here to fetch me? Are we finally going to be together? I'm so excited, but … I haven't packed … When will we leave …" My mind was spinning with the details but at the core it was obvious to me that I would be leaving with my sister, that I had been waiting all this time for her to come and fetch me, so we could carry on building our freedom, our dreams. My hands fumbled, my thoughts an excited mess.

Tannie Elna was beaming. "Thina, why don't you show your sister around? Introduce her to your house mother and all your friends."

"Yes, *Ya*Ziana! Let me show you my room!" I sprang from my seat and grabbed her hand, registering briefly that it was too thin, that my fingers had brushed over a cluster of pinprick scars.

"I have my own bedroom, *yaya*! And, ohhh, let me show you – I can read and write! Maybe you can even help me with my homework?"

*Ya*Ziana pulled her hand away to adjust her scarf.

We left Tannie Elna's office and made our way toward House Esther. The afternoon sun cast long shadows on the ground, the warmth still lingering.

In the garden we ran into the maintenance man, Oom Cleo, whose kind face lit up when he saw us. Everyone liked him – he always whistled while he worked.

"Oh, wow! You must be Thina's sister!" He leant in with open arms but *Ya*Ziana stiffened and her fingers dug into my arm.

"*Yaya*, it's okay," I whispered. "This is Oom Cleo. You don't have to be afraid."

But her reaction sent a jolt through me. How was I the one making her feel safe?

Was this the strong, fearless *Ya*Ziana, my sister who had held my hand and led the way?

*

My house, when we arrived, was buzzing with life.

Bianca was near the doorway polishing her shoes, and Natalie was sitting at the dining table focused on her lunch. Vero was lost in a computer game, her fingers flying across the keyboard. Tannie Santana was on the couch, a book in her hands, but she closed it the moment she saw us, and stood.

"Welcome, *Ya*Ziana! We've heard so much about you," she said in English, her smile warm.

Footsteps rained down the stairs as the other girls hurried to come greet my sister. Bianca, having put down her shoes, rushed in for a hug, and *Ya*Ziana smiled shyly, nodding.

"He-he-he-llo, h-h-h-how are y-y-you?" she stuttered. Her English wasn't perfect, but she could understand them.

I watched her struggle, watched her eyes widen as the girls surrounded her.

"W-w-wow, s-s-so m-m-many g-g-girls."

There was giggling at her broken words. I smiled, but something was gnawing at me. My *Ya*Ziana had been so full of life, so full of fire. But this person carried an invisible burden. And my sister had never stuttered.

"Thina, *gaan wys haar jou kamer. As julle wil, kan julle buite gaan sit en lekker gesels.*" Tannie Santana invited me to show my sister around, suggesting we could then go outside to chat. "*Bianca het jou skoolsak alreeds in jou kamer gesit.*"

"Thina, *vra vir jou suster – kan ek vir haar iets kry om te drink?*" Bianca chimed, offering a drink.

"*Water, asseblief*," I said quickly, and immediately felt a pang.

Why had I answered for *Ya*Ziana? Did she even want water?

I glanced at her, but she was just standing there, quiet. Not looking me in the eye.

Bianca nodded and went off to the kitchen, and I showed *Ya*Ziana upstairs.

"I c-c-can see you're f-f-finding yourself here," she said as she stepped into my bedroom. Her eyes scanned my things admiringly. "It's so beautiful, so neat, Popina." She settled onto my bed.

Excited, I opened my wardrobe and began showing her my dresses and shoes. When I held up one of my bras, she burst out laughing.

"Since when does my *popi* wear bras?" she teased.

"A lot happened while you were missing."

Her expression shifted from amusement to something deeper. She nodded, and then, without warning, burst into tears.

"I-I'm so proud of you, Popina." Her voice trembled. "You are ev-everything I-I ever dreamt of – and I know you will become even more."

Her words hit me harder than I expected. Warmth and sadness at the same time.

She was sitting on my duvet – so why did it feel like she was slipping away from me?

Bianca had left my school bag on the bed, and I reached for it, eager to show off all my hard work. I pulled out my maths book, flipping through pages of neat calculations, high marks in red pen. Then I opened my Afrikaans book, tracing my fingers over lines of words.

"See, *yaya*? I can read and write in Afrikaans and English!" I beamed.

One by one, I showed her my years of school reports and awards, the parts of myself I had built in her absence.

Her eyes shone with pride. And for a moment, just a moment, it felt like we were just sisters again.

Then there was silence.

"So, *yaya*, what is our plan? Should I start packing? How should I arrange—"

"C-c-c-calm down, Popina. I ... I j-just came to visit. Y-You ca-ca-aaa-aan't come s-s-stay w-with me."

Her words knocked the air out of me and my excitement drained instantly from my body. Tears streamed down her cheeks as I stared at her.

Why – after all these years, after *everything* – couldn't we be together?

"Popina, my Popina," she whispered. "I can't take you with me. I need you to stay here."

Her eyes locked onto mine and I swallowed hard, forced down the lump in my throat. I was trying to understand but I wanted to scream, to tell her I didn't care where we went as long as we were together.

"Why?" The word barely escaped my lips.

She tried to steady herself. "Y-y-you have a better chance of a f-f-future here. Th-they support you, they take care of you. Y-you have opportunities h-h-here that I can't give you."

She took a shaky breath.

"I'm a mess right now, Popina. I'm trying to find myself." Her voice cracked. "And I have a son ..."

A son.

The words hit me like a tidal wave.

"... He's only two years old ... I need to create a safe home for him first ..."

I barely heard her. She had a child.

She had built a new life – a life without me.

I felt my chest tighten as my thoughts raced back to the promise she had made on the phone. What happened to that future? She was leaving me behind.

I stood up abruptly. "You can't leave me here!" I shouted. "You promised! You said we would be together!"

Tears burnt my eyes, but I refused to let them fall.

"I've done everything you asked! I've been good! I've stuck to my schoolwork! I *waited* for you!" And now she was telling me she was choosing someone else?

"P-p-please don't shout," *YaZiana* pleaded softly. "Yes, we'll be together … but just in different places. You need to take this journey on your own now."

"What do you mean I need to take this journey on my own?"

She exhaled, as if searching for the right words. "I can't always be there for you, Popina …"

I shook my head. I was still standing, and my sister reached up to grip my shoulders.

"One day, everything will make sense. But for now, this is your path. No one can walk it for you."

Everything came crashing down.

"I'm scared, *yaya*," I admitted, and I let myself melt into her embrace.

And then she started coughing – a deep, dry cough that shook her whole body.

"Bianca!" I called, panicked. "Bring some water!"

Bianca rushed upstairs with a glass of cold water, which *YaZiana* sipped slowly as she steadied herself.

Her hands too thin. Her energy drained. Her eyes dim.

What had happened to my sister?

I stared at the sister for whom I'd waited so long.

"Thina, it's study time now," Bianca reminded. "No visitors allowed from 4 to 5pm."

YaZiana nodded. "I-I-I have to g-g-get going anyway," she said. "We'll speak over the phone, *popi*."

She reached for her bag, pulled out a plastic packet and handed it to me.

"I'm catching a bus back to Johannesburg tomorrow morning."

Curious, I opened the bag to find three pieces of KFC with chips and a small box of jewellery – earrings, necklaces and beautiful hairpins. My breath caught in my throat as I looked up at her.

She smiled.

"A promise is a promise."

2010–2017

Port Elizabeth, South Africa

32

Every second weekend I returned to my foster family, and each visit brought new experiences and lessons. The problem was that I was now struggling to adjust to a Congolese family because I'd been brought up Afrikaans! Some days were harder than others, but I constantly reminded myself of the bigger picture and the goals I had set for myself.

Meantime I repeated to anyone who would listen that I was totally fine with staying permanently at the children's home. Now that living with my sister was off the cards, I didn't want to go anywhere else.

"*Ek is baie gelukkig hier – kan ek nie hier bly nie tot ek agtien jaar oud is?*" I explained to Samantha – if I was happy, couldn't I stay till I was eighteen?

Samantha was kind but firm. "Popina, *jy moet verstaan – jy kannie hier vir die hele van jou lewe bly nie. Jy moet 'n familie kry.*" I had to find a family – so the answer was no.

Three months after my first visit, the foster arrangement became permanent and I moved in with Mama Naomie and her family.

After three years at the children's home in Despatch, saying goodbye to my own room, my friends, my school and especially my primary-school teacher, Mrs Ferreira, was heartbreaking. She had been my guiding light in those formative years, and letting go of her felt like losing a piece of myself. As I packed up my belongings, I promised myself that I would always cherish the memories I had made, the lessons I had learnt and the milestones I had reached. I would carry them with me as fuel for the pursuit of my dreams. It was time for a new chapter, filled with unknowns but also with the potential for growth. Even if the adjustment was challenging.

Because my foster family lived in Port Elizabeth, I had to change to Newton Technical School. Luckily, I soon found a friend in Margot, whose beautiful, sincere smile made me feel that I wasn't so alone.

School, however, was the least of my worries. At home, Mama Naomie was very strict and had high expectations, and I was kept constantly busy with chores and responsibilities. One of my tasks was to manually open the gate for Papa Kayi. Because the electric gate was broken and yet to be repaired, I had to get up when he returned home from working late at night. My foster father used the opportunity to take advantage of me.

"You came from rape, and you'll die from it too," he mocked.

I felt trapped with the fear of being sent away and losing access to school and a home. I couldn't bear the thought of uprooting my life again or dealing with more uncertainty. My need to survive and hold onto such fragile stability outweighed the courage I needed to speak out. I guarded the secret, pouring my energy into school and my friendship with Margot. I forced myself to keep going, step by step, to stay focused on my dream.

*

It was late afternoon, a few months after I'd moved in with my foster family. The golden light of the setting sun spilt into the living room where I was sitting in my school uniform, studying. But the room felt suffocating.

I hadn't seen Mama Naomie yet that day and I was surprised when she entered the room dressed in a loose black dress with a shawl draped around her shoulders. She was normally very stylish and well groomed, but her hair now was unkempt, her eyes red and swollen. She sat down heavily on the armchair across from me, clutching a tissue in one hand while the other trembled. For a moment she just stared at the floor. When she finally looked up at me, her eyes were glassy with tears.

"Thina," she began. "He's gone. Your papa … He had a heart attack this morning. He's gone."

The words echoed in my mind but I felt nothing. It had been months of getting up late to open the gate just so that he didn't have to get out of his precious car, only to endure his vile touch. He had reminded me time again that I was unworthy, that I didn't belong anywhere. And I had been trapped in silence – forced to endure his attention for the sake of food, a roof and the hope of an education. I resented him with every fibre of my being and I felt no sorrow.

Mama Naomie buried her face in her hands, her grief filling the room.

"It's not fair … He was our provider, our rock. And now …"

I couldn't bring myself to comfort her. I couldn't even muster the energy to pretend.

After a while, she straightened herself, wiping her tears with the edge of her shawl.

"Listen, Thina. With Papa gone, I can't do this on my own. The house, the food, the electricity – it's too much. I need you to step up."

Her words were like a slap in the face. Her own children didn't contribute a thing. I almost wanted to laugh at the ridiculous situation.

"I've heard that the Somalians in Korsten are hiring cleaners and shop caretakers. You could get a job there. You speak English well, and you're good with numbers. They'll take you."

My breath caught in my throat. "You want me to stop going to school?"

"Yes." Her reply was simple. "We need the money, Thina. This is our reality now."

I stared at her. After everything I had endured, she was asking me to give up the one thing I had fought so hard for? I knew then and there that I could not stay with this family. If I could work, I could earn my own money, pay my own food and rent, and take care of myself without her demands or being haunted by the memory of her vile husband.

No one was going to steal my dreams from me. No one.

I just needed a bit of time.

*

And I was only fifteen. To get a job I had to lie and say I was sixteen, and I walked from store to store handing out copies of my thin CV. I was determined to find something that would enable me to stay in school.

I saw that there was a lady opening up a new pizza takeaway in Westering. When I gave her my CV she told me she couldn't hire a teenager – she'd go to jail. I could see from her hairstyle that she was someone who liked to go out and about, so I told her I would do anything – clean, work the cash register, stock take and even close up the shop for her.

I got the job – and started as a part-time cashier. Most importantly, I could work and still go to school.

On weekdays I would rush straight from class to work a shift from 3 to 9 p.m., and on Saturdays my shift was twelve hours starting at nine. By the time I got home every day, I'd be completely drained. On Sundays I caught up on school projects and studying for exams, as well as the cleaning chores I still had to do for Mama Naomie.

By the end of every shift, my feet would ache and the smell of pizza would cling to my clothes – but I didn't care. I was earning money. Each month, I had to give what I'd earned to Mama Naomie, but I didn't give her everything. Without her knowledge, I kept some for myself and I started saving. Within a few months I had enough to tell Mama Naomie that I couldn't work for her. I'd come to this country to study, and I was leaving.

She wasn't that upset – she didn't think I would survive on my own.

"Who's going to pay your school and varsity fees?" she asked. "This is the life you have now, Thina, and you must accept it."

But I wasn't going to accept it. And I think this was the first time in my life that I had ever stood up for myself.

"Do what you want," she sneered. "But if you choose your studies, don't ever come back."

She knew my story and what I'd endured. I almost felt sorry for her for underestimating me.

*

I had a Xhosa friend who lived in Motherwell, and I asked if I could stay with her family for a while.

"Just give me a month," I said to her mom. "I'm going to find a place to rent and then I'll move out."

She reminded me that I was only fifteen – how was I going to rent something?

I said, "Just watch!"

The day I went looking in central Port Elizabeth, people regarded me as some rebellious teenager.

"Where are your parents?" they said. "Go home to your mother – I'll be arrested if I take you as a tenant ..."

Eventually I found a garage behind some flats in Military Road with a "To rent" sign outside. When I rang the bell, a white *oupa* came to open up.

"Hi," I said, "*hoe gaan dit* – how are things going?"

When he asked me how I knew Afrikaans, I said it was a long story. Then I asked about his garage for rent because I needed somewhere to live.

"You can't sleep in a garage – there is no door or anything."

I explained that I just needed a place to sleep and study – the rest of the time I would be at school and at work. "Sleep, go to school, go to work, study – that's my routine," I told him.

"*Hoe oud is jy?*"

I lied about my age that time – I told him I was seventeen.

"*Jy lyk baie klein vir sewentien* – you look very small for seventeen. Okay – it will be nine hundred rand a month."

I said I'd take it for seven hundred but he said no, because the garage even had electricity.

"But it doesn't have water," I countered.

"That's because people are not supposed to live here," he replied.

I could see that the old man didn't live there either so I said, "Look. Your garage won't be tampered with and I'll keep an eye on your flat over there too. You've got tenants, right?"

"Ja."

"If anything goes wrong – if I see that they are doing drugs or anything – I'll be the first to call you."

"Okay, *maar jy moet baie goed wees, 'n goeie meisie* – you must be very good, a good girl."

I said he had nothing to worry about.

He gave me the keys and I handed him seven hundred rand.

"I said nine hundred," he said.

"This is all I have."

He told me he'd be checking up on me once a week.

*

It wasn't much – the walls of the garage were raw cinderblock and the floor was concrete. But it was mine, a symbol of freedom, a place where I could take my first steps towards independence.

I bought myself a second-hand bed, a stove and a desk. Then I went back to my friend's house in Motherwell and asked her mother to come and see my new home.

"Ta da!" I said as we all trooped in.

"*Egarage!*" she screeched, but she must have seen there was no going back. She gave me her blessing and said she'd be checking up on me and that Samantha would let her know if I was ever not at school.

*

For the next two years, until I was seventeen, I lived alone in my garage. There was no insulation so winter nights were freezing, while in summer the heat was almost unbearable. The single light bulb that hung from the ceiling barely illuminated the space, and the sound of passing cars meant there was a constant hum of traffic.

It wasn't the life I had imagined, but at least I didn't have people abusing me. And I was at peace because I knew my mission: go to school, read your books, no boys and no drugs. Those had always been the rules, *Ya*Ziana's rules, and they had never changed. Living in that garage gave me something I hadn't ever had: control. I didn't have to answer to anyone.

It was the first place where I could just be, without fear of judgement or demands from others.

Even in the hardest moments, I held on to the belief that I was moving forward, building a life one pizza shift, one class, one day at a time.

33

The sound of the unanswered phone was like a relentless drumbeat in my ear, almost deafening despite the traffic noise outside my garage.

"Pick up, *yaya*, please pick up," I whispered. "Come on, *YaZiana*."

Finally, the click of the line connecting.

"Hello?" Her voice was faint and distant.

"*Yaya*, it's me – it's Popina!" I said, my words tumbling over each other.

So much had happened since we had last talked. After her visit to the children's home we'd stayed in touch, but not nearly as regularly as I had hoped. After escaping from Patrick's, *YaZiana* had got caught up in difficulty. She was working as a prostitute in Johannesburg, and drugs were once again part of her life. She told me she had tried to get other work, but with her lack of education and experience everyone had turned her down. She had no choice, she said – she had to eat. And she had a child to feed.

It broke my heart to hear her talk this way. We were now living in different worlds: she was trapped in a life that held no prospects while I was in matric, building my own freedom. And all the tiny steps were adding up: I was living on my own, and although it wasn't easy, I was making it work. Now all I could think about was bringing my sister to Port Elizabeth. I wanted to show her that she had choices, that she didn't have to be enslaved by her circumstances. I imagined us tackling life together – two sisters against the world, building a future where we could both find happiness and freedom.

"Oh, hi," she responded. She sounded rushed and distracted. I could hear noises in the background. Then a man's gruff voice followed by her sharp reply, "I'll be quick, okay?"

"*YaZiana*, are you okay? Where are you at the moment?"

"I can't talk long," she said abruptly. I could sense she was holding something back.

"Wait, listen!" I blurted out. "I've got a job now, and my own place. I was thinking you could move here, to Port Elizabeth. We can live together, make things happen, you know? Just you and me, *yaya*. We can finally be together again."

Her laugh wasn't warm or joyful. It was hollow, almost mocking.

"Popina," she said bitterly, "I can't live with you."

Her words hit me with force. "What? Why not?"

"I did my part," she said flatly. "This is your journey now. Your life. I told you."

Then the line went dead and I was left staring at the phone. Had my sister – my rock, whom I loved more than anyone in the world – just told me we were going our separate ways?

I didn't know what to feel or what to do. I just sat there with the phone in my hand, feeling a wave of emptiness. It felt like the world was instantly colder.

"Where do I go from here?" My voice cracked as I whispered my question into the void.

And then, like a flicker of light in the darkness, I saw a vision so vivid it felt like I was living it.

*

I am standing in front of a crowd. Someone calls my name over the microphone, and applause echoes around me. I can feel the weight of a graduation gown on my shoulders, the cap perched on my head. The image is so clear, so powerful – I can feel the crowd and smell its sweat and perfume, the flowers filling the hall.

So it wasn't just a dream – it was a prophecy.

Deep in my gut, I have always known that this moment would come.

*

"That's it," I whispered to myself, my resolve hardening. "I'm going to finish high school. I'm going to save every cent I can. And then I'll go to university. I'll make this vision a reality, no matter what it takes."

The loneliness I felt from being abandoned by *YaZiana* didn't disappear, but the cold ache lessened slightly because I had purpose again.

*

Afrikaans Vir Ons (Afrikaans for Us) – that was the name of my business.

In my last two years of high school I had noticed my black peers' challenges in learning to speak, write and read in Afrikaans. At the time, if a student failed their final Afrikaans exam, they could still pass the year if they had achieved an average of 75 per cent for their Afrikaans year work. I saw the opportunity.

"Stick with me, and by the end of the year you'll have a seventy-five per cent average for Afrikaans," I assured my classmates.

I set my prices: a hundred rand for writing an essay, a hundred and fifty to write an oral, and two hundred for reading lessons and lessons in mastering exam questions. Word spread like wildfire, and the demand was soon overwhelming. Students were desperate, and even those from neighbouring schools started to approach me. Suddenly, I wasn't just another student at Newton Technical – I was a legend, a mentor, a local celebrity. Business was booming, and the title "El Chapo of our generation" started making the rounds. It didn't bother me that the drug lord's nickname was not exactly a compliment. In my eyes, I was helping students get the marks they needed while I saved for university.

It didn't take long for demand to outgrow my capacity. I had too many customers, every entrepreneur's dream. I came up with a bold solution: recruitment. I started hiring Afrikaans students from other high schools to help with the workload, paying them a fair cut of the profits. With their help, my business became a well-oiled machine that served desperate students far and wide.

But with success came scrutiny. Teachers in my school started noticing that a growing number of students were excelling on paper but stumbling over basic Afrikaans in class. One morning in assembly the principal delivered a warning.

"We are aware of fraudulent activities concerning Afrikaans assignments and exams," he said, his voice booming across the school hall. "Let me make this clear – if we catch anyone involved, they will face immediate expulsion."

My stomach churned – the stakes had never been higher. The threat was not just to my business and my reputation, but to my future education. After much reflection, I decided to shut down the business. The burden of two jobs and mounting schoolwork had become too much anyway; exhaustion was clinging to me like a second skin.

One afternoon, I was having a conversation with my maths teacher. Mrs Richards reminded me of Mrs Ferreira – she was kind and sincere – and I found myself opening up about what was going on in my life. She listened attentively, her soft brown eyes never leaving my face.

"You're doing so much already, Thina," she said gently, setting down her pen. "Balancing all that while preparing for matric exams – it would be too much for anyone."

I nodded, my shoulders slumping. "I just don't see another way. I need to save and pay my rent and living expenses. I need to study. Somehow I need to make it all work."

She leant forward, a thoughtful expression on her face.

"What if you stayed with me for six months? Until your exams are over. You'd have a quiet space to focus, no distractions, no worries about rent or other responsibilities. After the final exams, you can always move out and figure out your next steps."

She had generously given me a chance, and I grabbed it with both hands. Determined to focus on my studies, I left my job at the pizza place and gave notice on my garage. I sold my single bed, desk and chair to a second-hand shop, and gave them my two-plate gas stove for free. All I had left was a bag of clothes and my school bag full of books. But moving into Mrs Richards's house wasn't plain sailing. Her son, Callam, was in my matric maths class, and the moment my classmates discovered I was living with him and his mother, it became a running joke.

"Whose your new sister, Callam? Look at you, adopting a black girl!"

Callam usually carried himself with confidence but the teasing chipped away at him. In the end, instead of standing up for himself – or for me – I became the target of his resentment.

"You're ruining my life," Callum hissed one day after class. "Why don't you just leave? I don't want you in my house, and I'll make sure you regret staying."

At home, he barely spoke to me except to hurl insults. I kept reminding myself of why I was there and that this was temporary. Still, I appreciated the respite from looking after myself, and I knew that no amount of bullying was going to distract me from my goal. At the end of 2013, I wrote my matric.

*

That summer of waiting for the matric results might have been the longest of my life. I had gone back to stay with my friend in Motherwell and eventually January arrived – and with it the moment of truth. Hugging my knees to my chest, I sat on the pavement outside the café that sold the local newspapers, waiting for it to open. The early-morning air was still cool, but my palms were clammy.

Had I studied enough? Was it my best effort? My future, my dreams – it felt like everything depended on what was in those fragile sheets of newsprint.

The first rays of sunlight hit the building, and I glanced up hopefully at the shop entrance. But the doors remained closed. More students joined, their faces mirroring my own anxiety.

Just when the anticipation was almost too much to bear, a skinny man emerged through the closed doors, holding a bundle of newspapers.

"Today's newspaper! Five rand!"

The crowd sprang to life, bodies pressing forward, each person scrambling to get a paper. Clutching the few coins I had saved for this day, I found myself rooted to the spot. This was it.

By now the poor newspaperman had been engulfed by the crowd. There were shouts of joy, anguished cries and the occasional heart-wrenching wail as each student discovered their fate. I caught sight of a newspaper lying discarded on the pavement, tossed aside by someone who had either confirmed their success or abandoned all hope.

I grabbed it and started flipping through the pages, my hands trembling.

The noise and chaos around me started to fade until it was just me and the newspaper. My fingers skimmed the pages, skipping over advertisements and headlines until I finally found it: Newton Technical School. I scanned the list, my heart pounding.

Straight to the Ks.

Khumanda ... Khumanda, Popina.

There it was: National Diploma.

I had passed.

"I passed!" My voice broke as I shouted to no one. "I passed!"

I looked around, searching for a familiar face, someone to share this moment with. But there was no one. No family. No friends. Just a crowd of strangers.

I dropped to my knees and the tears came hot and heavy.

The loneliness, the journey I had travelled to get to this moment. I cried for all the girls and boys in the DRC, who were always in the back of my mind.

I had to keep going; it was as simple as that.

Straight from the corner café I made my way to the school to collect my result sheet and matric certificate. Holding the envelope close to my body as if guarding state secrets, I headed straight to Nelson Mandela University to inquire about applications and tuition fees.

34

Naturally, I didn't have enough money to apply for university that year.

I decided to go back to the place that had changed my life for the better: Oosterland children's home. On public transport the journey took over an hour, but I took my matric results and asked them to help me go to university. They said they unfortunately didn't have the funds.

I didn't panic. By now I knew that every setback is an opportunity in disguise. If I couldn't start my tertiary education straight away, I'd spend the time preparing myself. So I got myself a couple of jobs – waitressing, looking after people's shops and doing stocktaking at Checkers. I started to understand how and where to look for these jobs, where to send my CV and when.

I was making money and at the end of that year I went back to the children's home for the second time.

"I've got five thousand rand saved," I said. "Can you help me?"

They told me again that they didn't have money to pay for my studies, and because I was a refugee, I couldn't get into the National Student Financial Aid Scheme.

While finding ways to earn the money I needed for university, I was determined to keep learning. So in 2015 I enrolled in a short course in electrical engineering at a technical vocational education and training college. I continued to work and finished my N6 diploma and graduated.

Then I went back to the children's home a third time to tell them what I had done. They said they still couldn't help me.

After that I sat and thought for a bit. I knew I couldn't continue to work like I was – I needed quick money so that I could save for university. So I looked around and thought, *What is missing in Port Elizabeth?* I'd noticed that most of the black women around me wore hair extensions, but they used synthetic hair that tangled easily and looked stiff and

unnatural. I decided to source a proper hair supplier and sell hair extensions.

I looked and looked online, and I eventually found a man who worked
at a temple in Tirupati in India. I called him, introduced myself and told
him I was looking for a hair supplier. He said yes, he could supply to
South Africa, but he only worked in dollars. I said I only had rands.

"It's going to be very expensive for you," he said, "but we can try."

Unlike my Afrikaans tutoring business, this one required an upfront
investment, and that meant taking a risk. The higher the risk, the bigger
the reward – wasn't that the conventional wisdom? By then I'd saved
ten thousand rand for university fees. I ordered a number of wigs from
overseas, and sent a significant chunk of my savings to this man in India,
hoping and praying that I wasn't being scammed.

Waiting for the arrival of the order was nerve-wracking. What if the
man was a fraud? What if the wigs got lost on the way? What if they were
terrible quality?

To my immense relief, none of my fears were realised. The wigs arrived
within a week, and they were wonderful quality. To advertise my business,
I started to wear them myself.

At the time I was waitressing at Angelo's Café, a restaurant on the pier,
and the other girls immediately started noticing my hair. But now I didn't
have any savings left for a down payment, so I gathered a group of twenty
girls, collected their money and sent it off to buy stock. It only took five
days to be delivered, and when I gave the girls their hair, they were really
happy and told their friends.

I called my business Urban Doll Factory, and slowly but surely it
gained traction. As my orders increased, I opened a Facebook page and
started posting videos of my clients. With every sale I was one step closer
to funding my education.

I had now saved enough to cover the application fee to study the next
year. I submitted my application and picked electrical engineering as my
first choice and information technology as my second. I got accepted for

IT, and chose to believe that there was a reason it had turned out that way.

The next obstacle was raising money for the balance of the tuition. I knew it would take too long to save enough money via my business – so I had to make another plan.

I returned to the children's home for the fourth time, and asked if they would meet me halfway in funding my education. I laid out my vision and the steps I'd already taken to make it happen. But the answer was still no.

Desperation breeds boldness, and I wasn't going to give up. I asked to speak to the director of the children's home, a man we called Oom Riaan. They said he was busy and that I needed to call in advance for an appointment. Instead, I simply walked to his office, knocked on his door and entered without waiting for an answer.

Oom Riaan was seated at his desk, looking slightly older than how I remembered him. And he was not alone – some other people were sitting across from him. They were in the middle of a meeting.

His eyebrows shot up as I burst into the room.

"Good afternoon, Oom Riaan. It's me, Thina," I said before he could object.

"Hi Thina," Oom Riaan said hesitantly. "Yes, of course I remember you." He was clearly confused, but he didn't seem angry. He glanced at his guests but they didn't say anything, and I didn't care.

Holding out my acceptance letter from the university, I blurted: "Oom, I've come to ask for help with funds to pay for my education. And I'm not leaving until I get it."

The room fell silent. Oom Riaan's guests stared at me. I wasn't sure if they were shocked by my audacity or curious to see what would happen next. It didn't matter. Without missing a beat, I laid out my case. I told him about my journey since leaving the children's home, my acceptance into Nelson Mandela University and my dreams of creating a better life. I pleaded with him to help me, promising that he wouldn't regret it.

"This isn't just for me," I said. "It's for every child who didn't make it, every voice that isn't heard. I have to succeed for them."

Oom Riaan leant back in his chair and studied me carefully.

Finally, he nodded. "Alright, we'll help pay your university fees."

Before he could take it back, I handed him all the necessary documents, including my acceptance letter. We agreed to have a follow-up conversation to iron out the details.

As I left the children's home, my heart pounded with gratitude and disbelief. I lifted my face to the sun. Sometimes, you just have to cast aside your pride and ask for what you deserve. Sometimes being bold is the only way to change your fate.

35

My first day as a student at Nelson Mandela University had arrived. The campus felt alive, bustling with the energy of ambitious young minds. The sprawling buildings with their clean modern designs stood like monuments of possibility, the walls whispering stories of transformation and triumph. I felt freedom in the salty breeze blowing off the ocean and in the crisp scent of freshly cut grass. The university's motto, "Change the World", was visible everywhere – and I could sense change in the air.

I was in awe of the large lecture halls, labs with rows upon rows of computers and the sheer scale of the library. Walking through the corridors, I felt both excited and intimidated. This was my chance – my golden opportunity. I would make the most of this gift. Of course, the goal was to earn a degree. But I also wanted to prove to myself, to Oom Riaan, to the girls and boys back home, to everyone who had crossed my path and everyone I was still to meet.

I wanted to prove that anyone can rise above their circumstances.

*

When I wasn't studying, I continued to earn money to support myself.

Urban Doll Factory was thriving. I was selling weaves, making wigs and offering wig-installation services to clients across campus and beyond. I had discovered that being an entrepreneur came second nature to me and I continued to look for more ways to turn my skills and passions into income.

Physical well-being and fitness was also something I felt strongly about. After being deprived of proper food for so long and then being addicted to drugs at the brothel, I had learnt the importance of taking care of my body – so I started creating fitness programmes for students and young professionals. In addition to the income, these programmes enabled me to connect with people and inspire them to prioritise their health.

During my first year of studies, the idea of telling my story transformed from a mere dream. Between lectures and assignments I started jotting down memories, piecing together the narrative of my life.

Through it all, my studies were always my main focus. I couldn't afford to fail or prolong my time at university: I had just three years and I had to make it count. Juggling multiple responsibilities and staying up late at night to study was tough, but I was determined to finish what I had started.

With every wig I sold, every story I wrote and every lecture I attended, I was one step closer to building my freedom.

*

Trrrrrrr-trrrrrrrr-trrrrrrrrr-trrrrr – finally the voice I longed to hear.

Three years later, *Ya*Ziana was in a much better place, although her circumstances were still far from ideal. She was dependent on her partner for a roof over her head and now had two children to take care of. But we were talking again.

I took a deep breath. "It's been a challenging time, *yaya*," I began, pausing to steady myself. "But guess what? I did it!"

Pride and relief swelled in my chest.

"I'm graduating next month! And I'd love you to be there."

There was a long pause at the other end of the line. I tried to imagine her face.

"Popina, that's incredible." I could hear she was trying to hold back tears. "I'm so proud of you. Not only because of your degree but because of … everything."

We talked for a long time, reminiscing, laughing and dreaming about the future. When I hung up, I felt profoundly connected to my sister.

And I realised that the story I needed to tell wasn't only mine – it was hers too.

Acknowledgements

There are twenty-six letters in the alphabet, and within those twenty-six letters lies the potential for limitless expression. Stephanie Kuhn and Nicola Rijsdijk, thank you for walking with me through this journey and making this book possible. By combining these twenty-six letters, we have brought this story to life.

I would also like to thank:

Amy Jones for having the courage to do the right thing.

Oosterland Youth Centre for being the place I needed to start again. My gratitude extends to all the social workers who were involved in my case and in my personal development.

Andrea Roux and your husband, Hugo Roux, I am grateful for your support while I wrote this book, which brought healing and acceptance and which allowed me to come to terms with what has happened to me.

There were times when I felt so alone and wanted to give up. Samantha Lamani, Evelina AkerLund and Pouna Monkam Nancy Dominique, thank you for being friends I could turn to, cry with and lean on for support and encouragement. Your presence has been a source of strength and comfort.

My teachers Mrs Gesila Ferreira and Mrs Cecilia Perrin, your influence in my journey has been profound. You inspired me to push myself beyond my limits, not only in my education but in everything I put my heart into. Thank you for your encouragement and belief in my potential, for your wisdom and support.

Tim Hewitt-Coleman, thank you for the time we spent together. You helped me see life from a different perspective and guided me toward a deeper understanding of myself. May you continue building freedom, and may Pebblespring Farm remain a place of magical mystery.

Marlene Fryer and the team at Penguin, this book would not have been possible without your belief in it. Your support gave it life, and for that I am deeply grateful. Thank you for not only giving this story a chance but also for giving a voice to the smallest ones who need it the most.

I could write a book solely with the names of those who have supported me and shown me love. I am profoundly grateful to each and every person who inspired me and gave me strength.

To my sister, I hold a deep and everlasting gratitude for all that you have done for me.

Whatever or whoever it was, a voice guided me through many dark moments and gave me the strength I needed to keep going. Knowing that I was being looked after, even in the most uncertain of times, gave me comfort and hope, despite the seemingly insurmountable challenges and hopelessness around me. In those times, I didn't know what the future would hold. I didn't know where I would be or what I would be doing. But I knew that I was not alone.

Last but not least, I thank God for being my saviour.